RENEW
Your Mind &
Transform Your
LIFE

Navigating Through the Seasons of Life

CLARA CONEY

Higgins
Publishing

Published by Higgins Publishing
1.877.788.5613 | www.higginspublishing.com

Higgins Publishing is committed to excellence in the publishing industry. The company reflects the philosophy established by the founder, based on Psalm 68:11,
"The Lord gave the word, and great was the company of those who published it."

Book design Copyright © 2017 by Higgins Publishing. All Rights Reserved.

The Higgins Publishing Speakers Bureau provides a wide range of authors for speaking events. To schedule an author for an event, go to www.higginspublishing.com.

Library of Congress Cataloging-in-Publication Data
Coney, Clara
Renew Your Mind & Transform Your Life – First Higgins Publishing softcover edition – November 2017
pages cm. 180   2017957399

ISBN: 978-1-941580-60-8 (Softcover)
ISBN: 978-1-941580-61-6 (E-Book)
ISBN: 978-1-941580-57-8 (Workbook)

1.   Christian Life: General
2.   Christian Life: Women's Issues
3.   Christian Life: Bible Study

For information about special discounts for bulk purchases, subsidiary, foreign and translations rights & permissions, please contact Higgins Publishing at 1.877.788.5613 or business@higginspublishing.com * Published in the United States of America.

"Therefore, I urge you, brothers and sisters, in view of God's mercy, to offer your bodies as a living sacrifice, holy and pleasing to God—this is your true and proper worship. Do not conform to the pattern of this world, but be transformed by the renewing of your mind. Then you will be able to test and approve what God's will is—his good, pleasing and perfect will." (Romans 12:1-2).

DEDICATION

Memories from the past can sometimes be painful and other times joyous. I dedicate this book to any woman or man who has struggled with painful memories from the past or present. Unfortunately, those we love and care about can inflict undeserved hurt. Relationships are challenging and complex, yet; all or most of us desire the companionship of a true friend. Memories live with us forever and how we process our thoughts have a significant effect on our lives, those around us and the decision we make.

If negative thoughts filtrate your mind and hold you captive to the past that is unpleasant, let this book "*Renew Your Mind & Transform Your Life*" be a source of empowerment and healing. Your life can be transformed and what was once a painful memory can become a stepping stone to a greater you. I also dedicate this book to those who caused pain to others. Perhaps they did not fully understand the impact of their words or actions. It is my prayer that their lives be blessed with hearts that become soft as clay in a Potter's hand.

Every life experience and relationship we encounter was designed with a purpose. As you navigate through your seasons of life, remember that some individuals are in your life just for one season. Hold on to the treasures that all people have and when you don't initially see beneath the surface, just keep searching because everyone has value on the inside.

CONTENTS

Contents

PREFACE

This book is a result of an assignment placed on my life that I did not initially welcome. Nor did I not recognize the need for change in my life. I knew that deep within I carried silent secrets from my past yet; somehow, I managed to ignore the still small voice that kept knocking at the door of my mental, spiritual and physical being.

I did not realize that the dry season in my life that I so carefully guarded and buried needed to be brought to the surface. Restoration and revival can never take place in our lives if we ignore our pain and sweep our hurt under the rug so to speak.

With no idea of where to begin, I realized that God had already started the process and I, in turn, had to make a choice; a choice that would free me from my past and a decision to walk with determination into a positive future. After a while, I came to the place where I began to look deep within and confront the fear's that were tormenting me. From within I began to view life with a new set of spiritual eyes as the journey on the road of transformation began.

I trust that as you read through these pages, you will take hold of God's love and unmerited favor that is available for you and decide to welcome the process of transformation. I spent many years being stuck when I didn't have to be. Therefore, I encourage you to read repeatedly the inserts in this book entitled, "Mind Changer(s)" because the battle is housed inside the mind. It's never too late to change your thought pattern. It does not matter if you've been rejected, disappointed, deserted, heartbroken or successful you can still make a choice to *"Renew Your Mind & Transform Your Life."*

Positive change is always beneficial, and with God's help you can *navigate through the seasons of life* and walk in Victory.

FOREWORD

The Christian life is to be lived as a *transforming life*. If we do not conform to the things of this world, we can be transformed by the power of the gospel of Jesus Christ. We cannot be transformed if we conform. If we live this life according to the dictates of the flesh, we will never experience the transforming grace and power of God.

The life of a Christian cannot be shaped by the image of this world. You can't have a renewed mind without the mind renewing 'Christ.'

Whoever controls your mind controls every aspect of your life. Allow the power of God to control your body, soul and spirit; today, tomorrow and forever.

God made it possible for us to be saved, not by deeds that we have done in righteousness, but according to His mercy, by the washing of regeneration and renewing by the Word of God. The Holy Spirit at work in our lives will affect our behavior, thoughts, feelings, and habits. The Spirit of God will produce healing, restoration, and deliverance. Through the works of the Holy Spirit, the world will see Christ in our lives.

"And I will ask the Father, and he will give you another advocate to help you and be with you forever— the Spirit of truth. The world cannot accept him, because it neither sees him nor knows him. But you know him, for he lives with you and will be in you. I will not leave you as orphans; I will come to you." (John 14:16-18).

Whatever we face in this life, God is with us and for us to renew our minds and aid us through the *seasons of life*. Is there an area in your life which requires transformation? Change is not easy because it requires a yielding of ourselves to the Creator. We must love God enough to say, "Lord you made me and I've decided to commit my future, family, health and everything that concerns me to you."

Change is both powerful and painful. Letting go of what we've become comfortable with is not easy. Change is powerful because it allows us to take hold of what has been given to us through the Holy Spirit and live it out. The impartation of the Holy Spirit and the power of the good news of the gospel is the antidote to anything that occurs in our lives. Once you decide to submit to God and take responsibility for change, the journey will take time. When we are honest with

God, He begins to change us from the inside out. When you decide to live according to God's plan, every area in your life will be affected. Transformation is something that takes place in private. In our secret closet, we develop our relationship with God. As we talk to the Father in prayer, He communicates to us through whatever avenue He chooses. God is not limited in the way He speaks. He may choose to speak to us through a Prophet, a word of wisdom or the beauty of His created world. As a surgeon performs an operation on a patient to clear blood clots from the heart so the Lord performs spiritual surgery in our hearts so that the power of His Word might flow in us.

Let your spirit be open daily to the move and voice of God. Block out interferences that come in with an attempt to steal whatever God has purposed for your life. Let the spirit of God rule and rein in your life. Letting others know that you have changed making your decision public. Don't worry if you fail or fear embarrassment; public commitments are powerful.

Conversion is something that must be seen in our lives. God's presence is seen in us when we walk in the light of His Word. Sometimes we are not aware of the light that shines in us. But it's evident in how we speak, act, and think about life.

Foreword

"But if we walk in the light, as he is in the light, we have fellowship with one another, and the blood of Jesus, his Son, purifies us from all sin." (1 John 1:7).

When we've done a thing the same way for so long, it can become a normality. The behavior may be dysfunctional, but the roots are embedded in the mind so deeply that it's hard to recognize there's a problem.

It is important that we see ourselves as needing a change. Making what is unconscious conscious and asking ourselves how do we see ourselves if we modify our behavior? Be an honest friend to yourself and admit the things you should change and be willing to have the courage to change.

Mind Changer

Courage: the quality of mind or spirit that enables a person to face difficulty, danger, pain, etc., without fear; bravery. Sometimes there's more than one thing that requires change, and it can become frustrating if we do nothing to modify the behavior. Being responsible for "one" change carries a tremendous amount of weight, therefore; we must make gradual changes step by step.

Maybe you keep going back to a relationship that only begins and ends in pain, but you keep going back thinking you can change the other person when the change must happen in you. Unless the heart is converted the path to change will be difficult. Be forgiving to yourself during the process of change. Mental punishment is rarely the answer for successful life changes.

Change *"To the fearful, it's threatening because it means that things may get worse. To the hopeful, it's encouraging because things may get better. To the confident, it is inspiring because the challenge exists to make things better."* (King Whitney Jr.).

It is essential to have a strategy in mind when planning your way to successful change. There is no magic pill. You have a part to play in the renewal process. You have the powers to counteract the attacks of Satan on your mind by using the weapons of pray and praise.

Knowing that the Spirit of Christ lived in me was the power source that thrust me forward.

"Behold, I give unto you power to tread on serpents and scorpions, and over all the power of the enemy: and nothing shall by any means hurt you." (Luke 10:19).

I encourage you to stay on the path to change. Be patient, positive and persistent on your pathway to God's promises.

Foreword

The route to your future requires you to leave the past behind and plant your feet in another direction.

"Those that be planted in the house of the LORD shall flourish in the courts of our God." (Psalms 92:13).

We can't always figure everything out, and we may never get the answers to our "why." However, in those times, we must turn our face towards our Father in heaven and say Lord order my steps according to your will. We will find peace along the way as we continue to trust Him. Every picture tells a story, and every life does the same. Christ's obedience, love, suffering, and honor are a portrait that should be painted in the hearts of all who know and believe in Him. In Him, we have eternal life. In Him, we have the forgiveness of sin. Because of Christ, we have within us the Holy Spirit. God in us is a constant reminder of how much we mean to Him.

With Christ presence, we can move to the other side of our pain. In Christ, we can do all things. As we reflect on the life of Christ, we see that He wanted to please the Father. As we live to please the Father let us reflect on His goodness. As we think about Him, we will live out every event and every situation with the knowledge that His love and mercy will sustain us. Our reflection of Him will help us in our daily lives. We can love more as we reflect on Jesus. We will forgive because we have been forgiven. As we reflect on the grace of God, our lives will be changed as we release our cares to Him even though we are challenged day by day.

INTRODUCTION

Winter, spring, summer, and fall are times of change. Whenever I look at the winter snow, springtime flowers, beautifully colored leaves on the autumn trees or feel the warmth of the summer sun, I'm reminded of how swiftly seasons change. We have no control over the changing of natural seasons that will take place whether we like it or not. Our lives will be altered by circumstances, experiences or consequences and we must be willing to accept the shifting of the seasons with grace.

"There is a time for everything, and a season for every activity under the heavens." (Ecclesiastes 3:1).

"Thus saith the LORD, thy redeemer, and he that formed thee from the womb, I am the LORD that maketh all things;

that stretcheth forth the heavens alone; that spreadeth abroad the earth by myself;" (Isaiah 44:24).

Whether are not we like change we must draw closer in our relationship with the Creator and move forward with determination, persistence, and endurance. Because God has chosen us we have confidence in Him that all things will work together for good. However, we may not always understand every circumstance. A songwriter once said, "We'll understand it better by and by." If by chance we don't get the answer to the "why" we must hold on to the "who." Who holds our today and tomorrow? Who keeps the waters of the sea in its boundaries'? The God of heaven and earth. The God who controls the Universe! He is the answer and has the answer to all things about us. Therefore, no matter how rough the winds may blow, no matter how dark the days and dreary the nights, we affirm that the Lord will make a way somehow. We can rest assured that He will continue to take care of us. He will calm the storms that rage in your life and speak peace to your heart.

What I've discovered about the times of life and what I've learned about seasons, in general, is that transformation can take place at any given moment. There were periods in my life when I felt like the winter months were endless. I was cold emotionally; paralyzed by the slipping away of unfulfilled dreams and broken promises. The blistering heat resulting from shame, rejection, isolation and hopelessness was like the scorching summer sun. I felt tired, torn and troubled. What could heal the thirst that left me emotionally scarred and physically dehydrated? When would I experience the fresh cool breeze of springtime? These are some of the questions I asked myself while looking out the window on that dreary winter day. Like high tides in the ocean filled with billowing winds, there were times when I felt like my life was spinning out of control. However; even though I was driven by the winds of time the hand of the Divine held me. When I needed to be released, God stepped in on time and renewed my inner man. I was free from a mindset that told me I was not good enough and that I was not wanted. I can express like Paul in the Roman letter, 'It is God's powerful way of saving all people who have faith.'

We cannot hold on to the past; we must let it go and excel like an eagle and fly to higher heights. We can soar high above the turbulence of time if we focus on what can be and not on what was.

"Trust in the LORD with all your heart and lean not on your understanding; in all your ways submit to him, and he will make your paths straight." (Proverbs 3:5-6).

The chilly winds of divorce, unemployment, low self-esteem, hopelessness and the unrealistic view of what being in the body of Christ was all about, left me spiritually dry and disheartened. I discovered a lot about religion, the do's and don't, pants, and dresses, makeup, offerings the tithe. Yet; I was perplexed, petrified and heartbroken while sitting in the sanctuary.

I felt as though I was wandering in the wilderness of Beersheba. Like Hagar and her child, while in the desert, I lifted my voice to the Lord and wept. It was in the wilderness that the Lord heard me. Whatever your wilderness experience might be God is near, and He is able to cause the gentle breeze of His extraordinary power to meet you where you are. One touch from the Master will turn you from a meandering path into a path of worship. We can build a place of worship in the wilderness. The Lord prepared an oasis in the desert and in Him I found a fountain that never runs dry. God is a drink for the thirsty and bread for the hungry. If you're thirsty and need refreshing come to the fountain filled with blood drawn from Emanuel's veins. Through it all, we must learn to trust in Jesus and give Him all the glory in all things. We are more than conquers through Him that loves us. He promised to be a shelter in the storms and quench our spiritual thirst when we find ourselves in desert places. He will refresh our souls and put a song in our hearts. He will turn trials into testimonies, pain into praise and regrets into rejoicing.

"The LORD is my strength and my defense; he has become my salvation. He is my God, and I will praise him, my father's God, and I will exalt him." (Exodus 15:2).

It's important to press each day upward and gain new levels of self-confidence, self-worth, and self-respect. Staying in the press means moving beyond the negative thinking that undermines you and makes you think you can't succeed. Positive thinking gives you the confidence to take up a new challenge and believe you can accomplish anything.

"I can do all this through him who gives me strength." (Philippians 4:13).

When we turn our face towards God He will take us to places we never dreamed possible. God will sustain you.

He will be a shield and hedge of protection for you against the fiery darts of the enemy. Do you want to go higher? My relationship with the Father is what kept me from being indefinitely committed to the psych ward while my relationship with religion is what kept me spinning in a web of confusion. Renewing my mind is what made the difference in my life. When a shift from religion to relationship began, the actual nature of God was revealed.

Introduction

Once there is an understanding of what God thinks of us and who we are in Him, life takes on a new meaning. God brings about renewal and transformation.

Here are some essential tools for *Renewing Your Mind & Transforming Your Life*:

- Reflecting on: A thought, idea, or opinion formed or a remark made because of meditation.

- Releasing of: Something that confines, burdens, or oppresses.

- Rejoicing in: A feeling or showing that you are pleased about something. How do you climb a mountain when the muddy slopes of despair cause you to slip?

- Reflect on: How far you've come and remember that you made it to the other side of your situation. We should daily affirm that the strength we possess is greater than our past.

- Releasing of: How do you experience the coolness of the summer breeze when the scorching sun of sadness and other negative thoughts make your mind a battlefield?

- Releasing it: Whatever it is that keeps you from being who you were created to be. Let go of un-forgiveness. Let go of love relationships that were never meant to embrace you.

- Affirming, 'I am fearfully and wonderfully made,' made to be challenged, changed and courageous. A new mindset does not happen overnight, and you are responsible for feeding your spirit. It is a choice that you can make, and I hope you will choose to begin anew.

Lastly, if you have reflected and released then there is nothing left but to:

- Rejoice In: Rejoice in knowing that you are free, free in Christ, free to love yourself and free to share in a relationship with Christ who is like no other.

When you see yourself in the light of God, there will be a power released in you that will change your life and your future. It is my prayer that this book will inspire, educate and equip your journey of *"Renewing Your Mind and Transforming Your Life."* Take this journey through the mirror of self-discovery. Allow the Holy Spirit to speak to you.

The person in the mirror has *power, purpose, and potential.* That person is you! Do you have a vision or dream? Allow God to show you His plan for your life. Expect great things!

Introduction

To know Christ is to know that *every season in life* is a time to honor God and bless His name. For the Lord is good, His mercy is everlasting, and His truth endures forever.

CHAPTER 1

Every Picture Tells a Story: My Reflection

A s the Coastal Line Moving Company pulled up into the driveway I realized that a chapter in my life was ending and another beginning. The most sacred union between a man and a woman was ending! Always and forever did not last. I believe that what God had joined no man could separate, however; separation was now my reality. As a new believer in the church, a place that once brought so much pleasure now was the place that brought much pain. After a long drive across multiple states and restless nights, I pulled myself together and made my way to Sunday service. It was a bright and sunny Sunday morning, and the chilly winds ripped through my thinly lined coat.

As my sister and I approached the church building, a friend said, "It's been so many years since I've seen the both of you together; can I take a picture of you and your sister?" Reluctantly, I agreed. Before the flash, I heard the word *smile*. Every possible emotion was tearing at the very core of my being, but somehow, I managed to muster up a slight grin. I was doing everything I could to hold back the tears. There I stood on the stairs of the church where I once vowed to love and to cherish till death do you part.

A part of me had died, but I knew that I was strong enough to make it. I just needed to pull determination into the now of my life. Within a few minutes, the disposable camera had produced the picture. There I stood, with swollen tired eyes, one huge pimple on the lower right side of my chin and a Bible tucked under my arm. If the truth be told, I didn't feel much like singing or praying that day. I was numb and dazed. During the service, I sat gazing at the preacher yet not hearing a word. I had to be in the place of worship because I knew that no matter how things were it would be by God's power for me to gain the strength to accept the things I could not change and move forward towards an unknown future. Even though my heart was broken, I knew that God was with me because He promised never to leave me nor forsake me. My mind and my soul were heavy laden, but the King of glory who is strong and mighty in battle was my help. I was in a fight. A fight in my thoughts and a war in my spirit, yet each day my trust and dependence were of God. The Bible that was tucked under my arm had found a lodging place in my heart. The peace that I needed could only be found in the Lord.

"Peace I leave with you, my peace I give unto you: not as the world giveth, give I unto you. Let not your heart be troubled, neither let it be afraid." (John 14:27).

As I stared at my photo later that night, I began to weep. I felt nauseous as the cry rang from deep within my belly. My words were silent except for the internal groaning. Even though I could not say a word, my longing reached the ears of God. Without blinking an eye, I looked at the picture and asked myself, who is this person looking back at me? Do I know her? Do I like her? Can I accept her? Could I have made better choices? Was it my entire fault? What happened to me? And finally, how do I begin to reshape my life and start over? The journey to healing took many years. As I look back on those early years, I can see the move of God in my life and the

31

purpose of the uphill journey. I've learned how important it is to reflect with thanksgiving even when the way is difficult. I've learned how to forgive and be forgiven. When we don't fully understand our plight in life or have all the answers, we must continue to trust God. I had to learn how to forgive and love myself because that old devil Satan kept whispering defeat, but God spoke His favor. There were times when all I could think of was other individuals and how they had contributed to my pain and the devastating results of a family being torn apart. The transformation began when I decided to turn all my cares over to God and take a serious look within. As the seasons changed so did I.

Sometimes you may never hear I'm sorry or forgive me. We have no control over others or how and if they acknowledge our agony. The only person we are responsible for is ourselves, and even then, we must allow the Holy Spirit to have His way in our lives to guide and direct our path every day. When we do reflect on our past, may it be through the lens of God's grace and mercy? There is comfort in knowing that life is a precious gift from God and with His help, we can begin again and be renewed in our spirit. All of us at some point take a journey down memory lane. We must never forget that where we are now is the result of the choices we have made after being directed by God. And regardless of what direction we took, God remained faithful to us! Because God

32

is upright, we are not paralyzed by a negative past that would have crippled our ability to be all that we are made to be. Instead, we take hold to the promises of God and step out on faith.

Mind Changers

"The Lord is my strength and my shield; my heart trusts in him, and I am helped. My heart leaps for joy, and I will give thanks to him in song." (Psalms 28:7).

"I press on toward the goal to win the prize for which God has called me heavenward in Christ Jesus." (Philippians 3:14).

We are the drivers behind the wheel of our spiritual, physical and emotional health and well-being. Decide in your heart that whatever you encounter on your journey you will address it with confidence in God's ability to restore, renew and revive you. If we reflect on the goodness of God, it will take us to places that foster gratitude, peace, healing, and giving of thanks. However, reflections can lead us to places of pain and regret, and that is a place no one should live in. When our minds are at a standstill in the areas of sadness and grief, we must quickly move from that state of mind by reading, praying and releasing contrary emotions of peace to God.

"You will keep in perfect peace those whose minds are steadfast, because they trust in you." (Isaiah 26:3).

As we meditate on the things of God, we must see ourselves in the image that is consistent with the Word of God and not twisted by the mirrors of the world. God's love for us included our mistakes, past, present, and future. God, the one who breathed life into us is the one who is qualified to define us. I believe that we were created to reflect His image, emulate His character and worship Him in spirit and truth. We are complete in Him and have been crucified with Him.

"I have been crucified with Christ and I no longer live, but Christ lives in me. The life I now live in the body, I live by faith in the Son of God, who loved me and gave himself for me." (Galatians 2:20).

All who we are and will become is because of what God did on a hill called Calvary. We are precious and peculiar children of the promise; Chosen to be Ambassadors and a royal priesthood. We are the salt of the earth and salt creates a thirst! We must be thirsty enough for God to create a longing in others who are around us. The light from within us is what matters not the light from without. The light from within shines in the darkness and radiates the power of God.

The Lord walked with me on my journey of self-discovery. When I didn't know which way to turn God guided my footsteps. He opened doors and shut others. I discovered who God was and that helped me to know who I am. Our help is in the name of the Lord, He is a strong tower, and in Him, we have a place of refuge. He protects us from the fiery darts of the enemy and sustains us when the blistering winds of life try to overtake us. Experiences; however, make us who we are and set the pace for our future. Reflections on who God says we are will launch us into a great future!

Mind Changer

"*I am God's Child: "But as many as received him, to them gave the power to become the sons of God, even to them that believe on his name.*" (John 1:12).

"The Psalmist says, I lift up my eyes to the mountains— where does my help come from? My help comes from the LORD, the Maker of heaven and earth." (Psalms 121:1-2).

As we lift our eyes to the Lord who is high and lifted up, we will see Him in all His glory, and His glory shall rain down on us with strength. We learn from our experiences. If we fail to learn from our experiences, we risk the chance of repeating the cycle. Men, women, single, married, rich, poor, young, old, healthy, sick, lower class, middle class, upper class; everyone goes through a time of transformation. From the moment of conception, our lives are being transformed.

Mind Changer
I am God's chosen:

"Blessed be the God and Father of our Lord Jesus Christ, who hath blessed us with all spiritual blessings in heavenly places in Christ: According as he hath chosen us in him before the foundation of the world, that we should be holy and without blame before him in love: Having predestinated us unto the adoption of children by Jesus Christ to himself, according to the good pleasure of his will." (Ephesians 1:3-5).

Love yourself and love others as commanded. Leave the past behind. Reprogram your mind through the Scriptures. Start dreaming. Start believing. Start living. Believe you have the victory over the past and hold each experience as a life cycle lesson. Just as darkness fades away to light in His own time, God will work things out for your good.

"Unto the upright there ariseth light in the darkness: he is gracious and full of compassion, and righteous." (Psalms 112:4).

When we accept Christ, He gives us His Holy Spirit. It is through the Holy Spirit that we are transformed moment by moment. His Spirit empowers us to live as new people through His power according to (Acts 1:8), *"But ye shall receive power, after that the Holy Ghost is come upon you: and ye shall be witnesses unto me both in Jerusalem, and in all Judaea, and in Samaria, and unto the uttermost part of the earth."*

Life begins anew when we accept what God says about us. When our minds begin to reflect on our past mistakes and failures, we must tell ourselves who we are in Christ.

God loves us, and during the transformation process, we must remember that we are in the Potter's hands. Change happens over time, and we must be at peace with where we are. Our past cannot hold us down but rather propel us into the promises God has for us. Circumstances or people may cause us discomfort, but we must take learn from our experiences and ask God to strengthen and teach us to love our enemies and do well to those who despitefully use us. Reflections and memories never change. We can modify the way we think about a given situation if necessary, but we can't change what happened or what was said.

Therefore, it's essential to be careful with our words. The love of God enables us to pray for those who dislike us for their reasons; ones of which we may never know or even need to know. Every season of our lives tells a story. It tells a story of God's goodness. It tells of *One* who is our constant companion, and it tells a story of our eternal future. When we look back, it's comforting to know that God has been with us every step of the way.

"The LORD is my shepherd, I lack nothing. He makes me lie down in green pastures, he leads me beside quiet waters, he refreshes my soul. He guides me along the right paths for his name's sake. Even though I walk through the darkest valley, I will fear no evil, for you are with me; your rod and your staff, they comfort me. You prepare a table before me in the presence of my enemies. You anoint my head with oil; my cup overflows. Surely your goodness and love will follow me all the days of my life, and I will dwell in the house of the LORD forever." (Psalms 23:1-6).

May we reflect on the goodness of our Shepard every day. Keeping our eyes on the Lord will allow us to sleep when turmoil is all around. The Holy Spirit comforts us in the midnight hours; His love protects us when the storms of life surround us. The Lord will give us a spirit of power, love and a sound mind when we rely on Him. When the enemy comes after us, the Lord protects us and sustains us through His love and keeping power. As a mother comforts her child, we too are comforted by our Heavenly Father, just like Mary Magdalene. Praise be to the Lord, to God our Savior who delights in those whom He created. Mary was the woman to whom Jesus had cast out seven demons. Early on the first day of the week, the Bible says that Mary went to the sepulcher while it was yet dark to see the body of Jesus. However, she found that the stone was rolled away and Jesus was not there. As Mary sat and wept, Jesus appeared to her and said: *"Woman, why weepest thou?"* Just as Jesus appeared to Mary, He will make Himself known to you in your darkest hour. If you desire to have a relationship with Him, He is always near. Reflect on the love of Jesus and then *Release* it in the world.

Real-to-Real Reflection… An Every Day Process

We reflect on a range of problems and situations all the time. What went well? What didn't? Why? How do I feel about it? We don't usually follow a formula for this; it just happens as feelings, thoughts, and emotions about something gradually surface. We might choose to do something differently, or not,

42

because of reflecting. Reflection is essentially a kind of loose processing of thoughts and feelings about an incident, a meeting, a day – any event or experience at all. As we *navigate through difficult seasons*, our relationship with God is what will keep us secure. When problems, pains, and perplexities overshadow us, we can rely on Jesus to be our refuge and strength.

Butterfly Scriptures

"These things I have spoken to you, so that in me you may have peace in the world you have tribulation, but take courage; I have overcome the world." (John 16:33).

"But the fruit of the Spirit is love, joy, peace, patience, kindness, goodness, faithfulness." (Galatians 5:22).

"Peace I leave with you; My peace I give to you; not as the world gives do I give to you Do not let your heart be troubled, nor let it be fearful." (John 14:27).

"Let the peace of Christ rule in your hearts, to which indeed you were called in one body; and be thankful." (Colossians 3:15).

"For He Himself is our peace, who made both groups into one and broke down the barrier of the dividing wall." (Ephesians 2:14).

" Have I not commanded you? Be strong and courageous. Do not be afraid; do not be discouraged, for the LORD your God will be with you wherever you go." (Joshua 1:9).

When I think of the goodness of Jesus and all He has done for me, my very soul cries out Hallelujah! I thank God for saving me.

CHAPTER 3

Who's That Girl in The Mirror? A Cover Girl!

M any people seemingly have everything and yet find themselves still empty on the inside. They pursue pleasure and dreams for happiness believing that the accumulation of riches and material possessions or popularity will satisfy them, yet they are lacking contentment and find themselves adrift in the sea of life—still seeking...still longing...still thirsting.

When you walk throughout the Cover Girl's beautiful home, everything is immaculate. The furniture has a high polished shine. The pillows are precisely placed on the couch, loveseat and ottoman. The floral arrangement accents the décor perfectly, and the fine artwork is displayed throughout the apartment. The kitchen counters are not cluttered, and the stove is shining as though it has never been used. There's a glow in the stainless-steel kitchen sink, and the floors are clean enough to eat from. The five-piece Broyhill bedroom set is *stunning!* The dark brown mahogany wood is accented by the creative artistry and detailed carvings. The bedroom curtains and comforter are filled with royal shades of gold mingled with multi-shades of purple and beige. The atmosphere is enhanced with the sound from *Boise* entertainment for listing pleasures, and a 72-inch *Samsung* flat screen, equipped with all the features that bring viewing delight.

Her nails are finely manicured, and her feet were pedicured to perfection. Every strain of hair has been carefully selected, and the hairstyle has been designed for a perfect look. Her handbag is a designer original as are the outfits she wears. She catches the attention of everyone when she enters a room. Who is this woman? What is her secret? The secret that she hides is in her closet, and as she stands at the open door of her walk-in closet she says: "What shall I do with this old blouse? I'll keep it in my closet. Oh, those shoes I've never worn I'll

46

keep them in the closet. All these books; some I've read and others are brand new, there all over the place; I guess I'll put them in the closet. I'll never be a size 8 or 10, all these clothes, well; I'll keep them in the closet too."

Her closet, filled with things! Things she'll never use, and some things long forgotten. She's spent countless years rummaging through stuff and spending thousands of hard earned dollars trying to satisfy the longing and emptiness she feels inside. As she sits in the middle of the living room floor surrounded by her things, she begins to sort them out only to discover that there is more she wants to keep rather than toss out. She had duplicated dresses, blouses, pants, coats and shoes. Many items still had tags on them.

Letting go of stuff is much like letting go of the past, it's difficult, uncomfortable and exhausting. Why is holding on to things, relationships and unhealthy memories so easily covered up?

Psalm 139:1-2 says, *"You have searched me, LORD, and you know you know when I sit and when I rise; you perceive my thoughts from afar ."*

Shame, rejection, fear, disappointment, lust, failures, *gluttony*, abuse, rape, are all the things she has become a prisoner of; she's locked in her closet of despair.

47

We can cover up who we are with an array of things. We can hide behind some flashy smile and beautiful clothes, but we cannot hide from God. God knows our thoughts. He knows our pains, fears and the shame we carry. God knows when we wake up in the morning and when we will lie down at night. Before we shed a tear, God knows. He knows when our hearts are heavy and the cares of life weigh upon us. There is no place that we can cover ourselves from His presence. Whatever we have done or will do is not unknown to our Heavenly Father. He already knows, and His love for us remains constant.

Hebrews 4:13 says, *"We are covered in His love and protected with His grace and mercy."*

There is no creature hidden from His sight, but all things are open and laid bare to the eyes of Him with whom we have to do. There are times in life when covering up a situation or hurt can seem easier than expressing true feelings. Depression, disappointment, and deception can be masked behind a smile. Cover-ups are temporary; eventually, the truth will at some point come to light. Adam and Eve tried to cover their sin in the Garden of Eden. (Genesis. 3:8). Adam blamed Eve, and Eve blamed the serpent. Some hide behind the statements like: "I'm blessed and highly favored, or, God is good all the time!"

Yes, we know that God is good and we are blessed; yet until you are honest with yourself and admit that you're hurting, healing will be delayed. *A mask hides the real you!* In the presence of God, our mask can be removed. We're accepted by God when others don't accept us. God loves us, and He will love us no matter what. We can come before Him with all our faults, all our fears, and all our failures. *Renewing our Mind and Transforming our Lives* is the work of God through the Holy Spirit. The stronger we become in His Word, the tougher we become! This toughness is not "hard" but a toughness that makes us equipped to handle the things of this world. We become strong in Him and through Him.

Galatians 2:20 says, *"I have been crucified with Christ and I no longer live, but Christ lives in me. The life I now live in the body, I live by faith in the Son of God, who loved me and gave himself for me."*

Because we are crucified with Christ, we make a conscious decision each day to walk in love, to forgive, to be compassionate and to let go of ill feelings. If you've ever used fading cream, you know that skin can be sensitive to the bleaching chemical. If you apply the wrong bleaching cream to your face, it will produce unwanted blotches, skin irritations and may require medical attention.

Our ears must be sensitive to the voice of the Holy Spirit. Cover-ups can block the voice of God. When our spirit is trying to connect to God in prayer, the flesh will try and intrude. It is essential that we be on guard to Satan's devices for we have learned that he comes to kill, steal and destroy. There is always a war going on between the flesh and the spirit. When pain is buried, unwanted negative attitudes can surface like pimples do when pores are clogged. Don't block the flow of the Holy Spirit in your life.

The blood of Jesus still has the power to restore. His blood is the cleansing agent that removes scars from your past, present, and future if you apply the healing when your spirit is lacking power.

There was a woman in the Bible that had a spirit of infirmity for eighteen long years, and women today who suffer from physical and emotional weaknesses. There are women whose flaws keep them from lifting their heads and walking in victory. What's keeping you bent over? What's keeping your head hanging down? Whatever it is Jesus is the answer for you. The Great Physician has been known to heal the brokenhearted, bind up wounds, regulate minds and cast out demons! He even opened the eyes of the blind. He can help you to walk again if the cares of life have crippled you. He'll open your ears to hear His voice. When you can't see your way through and don't know how you're going to make it trust God to lead you. God will not fail you! You can call upon Him when you're feeling down and depressed. Morning noon or night He will be available. Faithful is our God and worthy to be praised.

There is no God like our God. He reigns now and forever. Don't live under the covers of mistakes and failure. God does not make mistakes, and you are not a failure. Use your creative power and allow your experience to open you up to what you need to learn.

Every challenging situation has a lesson of value. Maintain a positive mental attitude during the transformation process. Regardless of what seems to be there is always good to be found.

Looking for the right is a form of renewal, however; we often must search for it with diligence. Hold on to your faith. When you have faith, you reinforce your subconscious to make your life move forward and flourish. You create your circumstance; your subconscious merely reproduces in your environment what you store in your mind.

Persistent Power - Be committed to change:
- Make daily affirmations.
- Consider your options.
- Choose what's best for you.
- Look deep within.

51

- Uncover the *Cover Girl* and let the *Real* you come forth.

Affirmations

"Ye are the light of the world. A city that is set on a hill cannot be hid." (Matthew 5:14).

"For ye were sometimes darkness, but now are ye light in the Lord: walk as children of light." (Ephesians 5:8).

"When Moses came down from Mount Sinai, he had the two tablets in his hand, and he did not know that the skin of his face was ablaze with light because he had been speaking with God." (Exodus 34:29).

"For thou art my lamp, O LORD, and the LORD gives light unto my darkness." (2 Samuel 22:29).

Cover Girl

- **Daily Cleansing:** (Daily washing removes dry particles that hide beneath the surface). Through daily spiritual cleansing we purify our minds and destroy toxins that can contaminate our spirit.

"But if we walk in the light, as he is in the light, we have fellowship one with another, and the blood of Jesus Christ his Son cleanseth us from all sin." (1 John 1:7).

Recognize: We must accept the fact and be aware of our need for daily cleansing. Our consistent self-assessment will allow us to be true to the reality of "self." Toxins can accumulate in our lives causing dysfunction and disease. Cleansing activates the mind to purge itself from toxicity and replenishes our system.

Release: We must not hold ourselves hostage to the past. You must release yourself and others from whatever was done or said that hurt you.

Surface Peel: The skin is a protective seal for the body. Our spiritual "skin" can become infected and discolored if it lacks spiritual nutrients. Strip off defeating labels that don't define who you are in Christ.

Surface: An outside part or layer of something.

Peel: to strip off an outer layer of/to remove by stripping (peel the label off the can).

Mask:

- Never cover up your true identity. Except who you are. Be honest with God about how you feel. God already knows the areas in your life that require change. We can't conceal anything from God because He knows all about us and He loves us in spite of ourselves.

Re-balancing:

- Being out of balance is unhealthy and can affect every part of your life. Our lives are impacted by constant change. The result of imbalance will increased stress and the conditions that are associated with it. Balance begins with our relationship to self and our creator. Thinking about things too much is exhausting. Thinking negatively will bring you to a place of nothingness, being in the present only with our body but not with our mind, is surly a sign that things need to be re-directed and in order to bring stability in your life.

Daily Nourishing/The Ultimate Protection

- Why is it important to invest daily in your life?

"But the Lord is my refuge; my God is the rock of my protection. You are valuable to God. Cover yourself in your relationship with God and allow his care to be your ultimate protection." (Psalms 94:22).

Butterfly Scriptures

"I will give thanks to you, for I am fearfully and wonderfully made; Wonderful are your works, and my soul knows it very well." (Psalms 139:14).

"Worthy are you, our Lord and our God, to receive glory and honor and power; for you created all things, and because of your will they existed, and were created." (Revelations 4:11).

"For I am convinced that neither death, nor life, nor angels, nor principalities, nor things present, nor things to come, nor powers, nor height, nor depth, nor any other created thing, will be able to separate us from the love of God, which is in Christ Jesus our Lord." (Romans 8:38-39).

"When I consider Your heavens, the work of Your fingers, The moon and the stars, which You have ordained; What is man that You take thought of him, And the son of man that You care for him? Yet you have made him a little lower than God, And You crown him with glory and majesty." (Psalms 8:3-8).

"*For you formed my inward parts; you wove me in my mother's womb.*" (Psalms 193:13).

"*The Spirit of God has made me, and the breath of the Almighty gives me life.*" (Job 33:4).

CHAPTER 4

Color Your Rainbow: Stained Glass Windows

Worship service is a time of praise and adoration to the Lord. We praise God for who He is and for what He has done. Worship is a time to join in harmony with the songs of the choir and to anticipate the move of the Holy Spirit through the preached Word. We dance before the Lord, lift holy hands and bow down in His presence. One Sunday morning as I sat in the sanctuary I turned my head towards the stained-glass windows. There is a quiet beauty in the vast colors and shapes of the window panes that I've always admired. There is a moment of tranquility when I see the sunshine against the multifaceted colors. The beauty found in stained-glass window panes is much like the beauty found in each of us. One Sunday as I looked closely at the stained-glass windows I pictured in my mind the figure of a woman with her hands lifted. In the center of the panes, it appears there was a flaming fire being released from her belly. The burning fire caused me to think of the power each of us has within. The power that burns inside can move us to lift our hands, shed a tear, shout Hallelujah or just stand in awe.

I thought for a moment how stains from my past were turned into something beautiful. Something lovely can be birthed out of our pain. Something marvelous can be released, renewed or restored from the stains that discolor our canvas. There is a place in God for which we were created to give Him glory and declare His name in the earth. Stained-glass windows do not allow us to look on the outside, however; the beauty can be seen from the outside.

Within us, there is so much that the Lord has deposited. What has been invested in us must be birth from us. So often we lose our way by looking at others and expecting them to do for us what only God can do. I know because that was me. How did I make the shift? *I said yes* to the Lord and waited for

Him to equip me for His service. Our yesterdays may have many shades and hues. There are days when we glisten like gold and days when fiery red shines brightly.

In John chapter 1 the gospel speaks of light, and that light is Jesus. *Jesus is the light of the world.* His light shines in the darkness, and His light must shine in us. God created the universe. Without Him, nothing would exist. He speaks, and things appear. From darkness, He brings light. He makes something out of nothing. Everything that we are and everything that we shall be is a result of who Christ is. Without the indwelling of the Holy Spirit, we are empty, lost and lonely. We have no hope, we have no power, and we have no vision. The light of Christ shows us the way; shields us from harm and shelters us from the raging storms of life. The life of Christ is the light for the world.

"In him was life; and the life was the light of men." I want the light of Christ to shine in the world through me... don't you?" (John 1:4).

"Then spake Jesus again unto them, saying, I am the light of the world: he that followeth me shall not walk in darkness, but shall have the light of life." (John 8:12).

"For God, who commanded the light to shine out of darkness, hath shined in our hearts, to give the light of the knowledge of the glory of God

in the face of Jesus Christ. Our lives can be a reflection of a beautifully painted stained glass window with the light of Christ at work within. Because of the light of God living in us there is no stain that cannot be removed." (2 Corinthians 4:6).

"Let your light so shine before men, that they may see your good works, and glorify your Father which is in heaven." Struggles are a part of our journey. Develop love for yourself. Don't condemn yourself learn to love you. Grow through your struggles; grow through them and move forward." (Matthew 5:16).

"For thus says the high and exalted One Who lives forever, whose name is Holy, 'I dwell on a high and holy place, And also with the contrite and lowly of spirit In order to revive the spirit of the lowly And to revive the heart of the contrite.'" (Isaiah 57:15).

"O LORD, You are my God; I will exalt You, I will give thanks to your name; For You have worked wonders, Plans formed long ago, with perfect faithfulness." (Isaiah 25:1).

CHAPTER 5

Think I'd Better Let It Go: Silent Secrets

Secrets can be carried for years, and there are secrets some people die with. Some secrets are painful and can destroy lives and steal futures. Life will throw curves your way; the journey in this life is not straight; there are many turns we take, many pitfalls and some dead ends. Some curves we can detour, others hit us head on. Internalized hurt can hinder your progress and your relationship with others. Don't become a prisoner of the past... locked-up behind the bars of your yesterday.

Silent: Unspeaking, mute, quiet, still, wordless and speechless.

"I have been silent a long time. I have been quiet and restrained myself. Now I will cry out like a travailing woman. I will both gasp and pant. Secret." (Isaiah 42:14).

Secret: Kept or meant to be kept private, hidden (kept out of sight/blotted out), concealed (covered up).

"For in the day of trouble he will keep me secretly in his pavilion." (Psalms 27:5).

We often said, 'I will keep silent even though; I'm broken, battered and emotionally beat down. You won't get a word out of me.' God's ears are open for your need to 'Release' your 'Silent Secrets' to His care. Our silence is often filled with fear, doubt, anxiety, hopelessness, and confusion. The desire to radiate the reflection that beams across the horizon are somehow trapped in a maze of broken promises and shattered dreams. Silent secrets can be like an unending nightmare.

62

Monsters from the past creep into the hidden spaces of one's mind and block the flow of sunlight. It's time to let the sun shine in and display the amazing treasures that are inside of you.

Breaking the barriers of silent secrets is not easy but extremely necessary for moving forward. If you're struggling with memories from the past whether they are with family, friends or enemies, it's time to let it go. It's times to release the thoughts that have held you captive.

~

This chapter on stained-glass windows and silent secrets has been designed to help you release the past and step into the future that God has for you. *It's time to shift!* The mind is somewhat like a computer; it stores our experiences. On the computer keyboard, there are keys marked: escape, delete, lock, control, alternate, enter, pause, break, insert, shift and backspace to name a few.

Escape: to avoid / to get free of: break away from/ to fail to be noticed or recallable by / mean to get away or keep away from something.

Delete: to eliminate especially by blotting out, cutting out, or erasing (delete a passage in a manuscript) (delete a computer file) you can delete a file on the computer but remember information can be saved on the "Hard Drive" as a permanent file.

Lock: a fastening (as for a door) operated by a key or a combination

Control: to direct the behavior of (a person or animal): to cause (a person or animal) to do what you want: to have power over (something): to direct the actions or function of (something): to cause (something) to act or function in a certain way.

Pause: a temporary stop: a period in which something is stopped before it is started again: a control that you use when you want to stop a recorded song, movie, etc., for a short time music.

Break: to separate (something) into parts or pieces often in a sudden and forceful or violent way: to cause (a bone) to separate into two or more pieces: to open suddenly especially because of pressure from inside.

Insert: to put or thrust in; to put or introduce into the body of something: to set in and make fast; especially: to place into action (as in a game) intransitive verb of to put or thrust in.

End: the point at which something no longer continues to happen.

Backspace: Shift to change direction, to exchange for or replace by another, to move or to cause (something or someone) to move to a different place, position, etc.: to change to a different opinion, belief, etc.: To go from one person or thing to another. Fear grips us and renders you helpless, powerless, without confidence and paralyzed. Fear is not from God.

"For the Spirit God gave us does not make us timid, but gives us power, love and self-discipline." (2 Timothy 1:7).

Not all things that have occurred in our lives can be shared with others, but we can tell God everything. Silent secrets can eat at the very core of one's being and make you miserable. A facial expression can denote silence. Gazing, a mind may be spinning like a windstorm, but one cannot express what's on the inside because of fear, rejection or shame. When we consider the computer keyboard in conjunction with silent secrets let's discuss the below:

Real-to-Real

- He told me I'd better never tell anyone so for years I lived with silence secrets. My mother's boyfriend touched my private part as I walked by; I didn't mention it until I was an adult. Why did I hold it in for so long?

- He beat me up again… but, I love him. I know he's a liar and never keeps his promises so why do I keep giving him control over my body?

- I work and pay most of the bills, but I'm not lonely at night. He doesn't speak to me in public settings only when we're alone.

- I saw my mother sleep with men so, why can't I?

- I ate the whole cake; I should feel better.

- My boyfriend sold me to his friends for drugs. I need drugs.

- I know he's cheating, but I have a home and kids.

- He'll always be my husband even though we're divorced.

- Keep quiet.

- Don't tell anyone.

- You can handle it alone.

- It's nobody's business anyway.

- I'll figure it out on my own.

There's a turning point that each of us must take when it comes to being honest about our pain. Pain is real, and it won't go away by itself. Face the facts. It may be painful; you may have to cry, but identifying your feelings helps you to release others whereby allowing you to release yourself.

Fallen Fragments & Forging Ahead

- Escape- Break-a- way from negative energy.

- Delete- anything that corrupts your life.

- Lock- Protect yourself from intruders.

- Control- Never release your power to anyone else.

- Pause- Take time to be still and seek Devine direction.

- Break- Unhealthy thinking patterns.

- Insert- Be empowered each day by applying the scriptures and prayer to your life.

- End- Separate yourself from unhealthy relationships (male or female).

- Backspace- Remember how far you have come and continue to grow in some area of your life.

CHAPTER 6

Building Bridges from Broken Pieces: Shattered

Dreams

How do we build our lives when our spirits have been broken and our dreams shattered? There's a bright side to brokenness, and if we search, we will find it. In a moment in time, our lives can be drastically changed. Our peace can we wiped away like the sand on a beach when the high tides come bursting through, and times when our dreams can be ruined by one bad choice or tragic event. When our spirits have been crushed, broken or shattered, we need to find a place of refuge. You can reshape your future by picking up the shattered pieces of your life and putting them in the Potter's hand.

Story #1

Has a glass ever slipped out of your hand and fell to the floor? Once glass hits the floor shattered fragments scatter all over the place, and it's difficult to clean up the mess because the residue is not easily seen. Then one day I was walking barefoot on the floor, and a tiny piece of glass entered my foot. When I stepped on the fragment of broken glass in my kitchen an area on my foot began to bleed. At first, I could not see the glass, but I could feel the sharp edge. I took a pair of tweezers and pulled the piece of broken glass out and covered the wound with a bandage. The pieces of glass were small but still caused me to bleed. Just like the traumatic experiences in our lives. Sometimes we open the door of our lives and allow intruders to run off with our "stuff." Left behind are the fragments of depression, embarrassment, discouragement and remorse. Anytime we bare our souls to someone we risk the chance of being hurt. We must guard our hearts otherwise; we become victims of self-induced pain. Yes, we slip and fall in life, we make mistakes, but we can't remain still and unmovable. When we allow God into our situation, we will discover that He has always been there waiting for us to let Him enter in. You may be on the edge of a breakthrough and not even know it. If the Holy Spirit lives inside of you, He will guide you through the areas in your life that need healing. No matter the size or complexities of your situation know that God is willing and able to bring you out and see you through.

Proverbs 3:5-6 says, *"Trust in the LORD with all your heart and lean not on your own understanding; in all your ways submit to him, and he will make your paths straight."*

Story #2

A few years ago, my sister bought me a lovely figurine for Christmas. The figurine was two sisters standing side by side, and the older sister has her arm around the younger sister. The figurine represents my sister and me, and it is exceptional. One night as I was cleaning I moved the chess drawer, and my lovely figurine fell to the floor and the head of the older sister shattered into several broken pieces. I tried to put it back together, but I was unsuccessful, however; I will not give up. I have all the pieces in my possession, and it's just a matter of time before its back together again.

There is a story in the Bible about a girl named Tamar in 2 Samuel 13:1-19, whose life was stained by the lust of her half-

71

brother Amnon and her dreams shattered. Ammon fell in love with Tamar and became frustrated to the point of illness because he wanted her so badly and she was a virgin. So, Ammon pretended to be ill and asked his father to have Tamar bake some cakes and bring them to him.

When Tamar had baked the cakes and presented them to Ammon, he refused to eat them and ask Tamar to bring the food to his bedroom that he might eat them out of her hand. But when she took them to him, he grabbed her and said, "Come to bed with me, my sister."

Ammon raped Tamar and hated her afterward. Tamar's life was changed, and the innocence and status she once valued could never be regained.

Devastating things will happen in our lives leaving behind a feeling of brokenness. When something we hold dear to us is taken away from us by force, it can cause a sense of shame, fear, and abandonment. We may not always understand why God allows such things to happen as He did in Tamar's life and our lives. However, at times of despair when it seems all hope is gone, we can only through the help of the Holy Spirit be restored. God can use us and our brokenness and shattered dreams to help someone else. Our Heavenly Father can transform lives that have been tarnished by the sins of others against us or by our own choices. Don't let guilt overtake you if you fell into sin. Be grateful that God sustained you. His

72

grace brings us over and pulls us through the valleys and the dry places. He will take the pain of our situation and turn it into praise. Praise is indeed birthed through agonizing and painful events. God has a purpose for everything we encounter in this life.

In Mark 5:24–34 and Luke 8:42–48 we find the story of the woman with the issue of blood. What we know about the woman is she suffered from a bleeding disorder for twelve long years. She had spent all her money on many physicians, and instead of getting better she became worse. Jewish Law declared her to be unclean due to her bleeding issue. She would not have been allowed to enter the temple for Jewish ceremonies. Anything or anyone she touched became unclean. She was in the crowd pressing around Jesus which means that each person who bumped into her became unclean. The woman was desperate for a miracle. When she heard about Jesus, she came up behind Him in the crowd and touched His cloak. She believed that if she could just touch the hem of His garment, she would be made whole.

As soon as the woman touched Jesus, she bled no more. Instantly, Jesus does what others had tried to do in twelve years but could not. The same power that flowed in the woman's life through Jesus can flow through you. The blood of Jesus heals, delivers and will mend your brokenness. Life's responsibilities have the tendency to cause pressure and stress. Daily we need a touch of God's sustaining power to see us through. The Word declares that *"His strength is made perfect in our weakness."* (2 Corinthians 12:9b).

When our hearts are broken, we need a touch. When death, disappointment, and despair come, we need the real love of Jesus. Don't allow your past brokenness to keep you in a negative space. Be mindful of the need to spend quality time with God. Learn from your past, so you don't have to repeat lessons repeatedly. If you keep thinking positive and remove yourself from the negative energy, you will be on your way to a new beginning. Flowers don't grow in the winter, but snowflakes purify the earth so that when the time comes for the flowers to bloom the soil has been prepared. You're being prepared for something great!

Be faithful steadfast and unmovable. You're in the hands of the Potter, and He can form anything to His liking. He is the repairer of broken pieces. God knows how to bring it all together. If God can call dry bones to come together, He can put you back together again. At times in our lives we become anxious for something or someone and as a result make poor decisions. All at some point will suffer from self-inflicted wounds. It's been said that immediately after a finger is cut the area begins to purify itself and the healing begins. We must quickly identify the cause of our hurt. Don't cover up your pain. Turn that experience around. Speak aloud what you feel;

74

recognize it, accept your responsibility and make an action plan.

If you find out that your here and now is unbearable and makes you hopeless, here are some options: remove yourself from the situation, change it or accept it. When everything seems to be at its darkest, remember that the gloomiest hour is just before the morning; the dimmest hour is exactly the time for you to shine, like the star in the night you can shine.

Everyone born in this world has a story to tell, men women, boys, girls, the rich, the poor, the sick and the well. You're not alone. There is life running through your veins. You are unique in the sight of the Lord. There is no one else like you in the entire earth. Your *DNA is what makes you distinctive!* It accounts for why you resemble your parents, and it distinguishes you from everybody else. You may not understand why you behave or feel the way you do, but sometimes it just may be connected to your bloodline.

Silent unspoken secrets tucked in our mind resulting from our bloodline that hinders us must be unleashed. In this life, there will be situations that shatter us to the core of our being. How will we deal with these broken pieces, it is never whether they will come because they will?

"We need to realize that our path to transformation is through our mistakes. We're meant to make mistakes, recognize them, and move on to become unlimited." (Yehuda Berg).

CHAPTER 7

Cutting the Strings: Release It & Let It Go

There is a story in the Bible of an un-named woman who had a thirst that only God could satisfy. She was not the shy, retiring, subservient woman much admired in traditional cultures. She is a woman in pain, argumentative, bitter, tired, lonely, rejected and spiritually bankrupt. Each day when it was the hottest, she would carry a heavy water pot to a well to satisfy her physical thirst and that of the man she was living with. Jesus comes to this woman as the seventh man in her life asking for a drink of water. I can imagine that this woman at the well got tired of carrying the water pot to the well day in and day out. The roads were dusty and long, and the water pot was heavy that she lifted upon her shoulders. I can relate to the Samaritan woman, what about you? Sometimes in our walk with God; we get tired, frustrated, lonely, fed up, desire companionship, intimacy and love; yet, we have the tendency to seek satisfaction in material things or weak relationships. If we strive to fulfill our desires with momentary means or *in the arms of flesh*, we set ourselves up for disappointment. If the Divine does not drive your desires, you come up empty every time. While visiting my 82-year-old mom last week, I asked her what she knew about the Samaritan woman. A few minutes afterward she replied; 'I can explain the story, God is everything to me!'

Physical water will always require replenishing. That's what Jesus told the Samaritan Woman in so many words. But the Living Water which is the Holy Spirit will help you to cope in dry seasons. When you're in a dry valley, God can turn dry places into an oasis. When the wind of the Holy Spirit fills the sanctuary through the preached Word take a deep breath and come alive. God will bring you out of the valley so you can walk in victory! My testimony is not that I haven't done anything. I've done much, but God still found a way to get me on the right path and make me useful. When everybody else threw me away and kicked me to the curb, God went to the curb and picked me up and said that I had a purpose, and He was going to use me.

There is a Fountain Filled with Blood

There is a fountain filled with blood,
drawn from Emmanuel's veins,
and sinners plunge beneath that flood
lose all their guilty stains."
(William Cowper).

I'm a sinner saved by Grace, and I need an endless flow of Living Water. The woman at the well had her sins "washed away" by Jesus. The story shows that Jesus offers Divine mercy in the Living Water of grace, which washes away sins and cleanses souls. She went to the well with her issues, but left them there and went to evangelize. The blood of Jesus *cleanses, delivers and saves!* It goes where I can't, see's what I can't, and covers what men won't. Lord, into your hands we commend my spirits, transform our minds and change us from the inside out. In Jesus's name. Amen.

The message of the Bible and the message in this chapter is "Our God is a God you can have a relationship with.

Everything you need and desire can be found in Him! We are not saved by a list of traditions but by a personal relationship with God through Divine forgiveness.

What does it mean to forgive?

To pardon or release. The act of excusing a mistake or offense. Ceasing to feel resentment or anger. Forgiving is a journey. The road to forgiving is not smooth, but if you stay on the path, the experience will produce wisdom. Don't get discouraged if you must go through the forgiving process repeatedly. Each step you take towards forgiveness is working together for your good.

Don't become paralyzed by your hurt:

- Identify your feelings (write them down).
- Don't expect the person who hurt you to apologize.
- Forgiveness is the key that unlocks the prison door and sets you free.
- Forgiveness is a choice; a choice that requires lots of determination.

Sometimes, the person we need to forgive is ourselves. Forgiving yourself is an opportunity to free you of pain and anger that has built up over time. Forgiveness moves you from focusing on a past hurt into the present. You may not forget the severe event, but you can move on with your life. This choice to forgive yourself may not be a one-time event and may take some time to do, but as the hands of a clock continue to turn you will find yourself living without the familiar pain you once carried.

Forgiving yourself may not be easy, but the alternative is choosing to live with the residue of bitterness and resentment toward yourself. Holding on to past hurt and anger does nothing but cause you stress! You are not hurting the other person by harboring these emotions. You are only hurting yourself. Give yourself the relief you deserve and forgive those who have hurt you. Failure to forgive ourselves can result in continually being hurt by unresolved issues. If someone has hurt you, of course, you should forgive them, but you don't have to allow them to hurt you again. Low self-esteem and low self-worth are self-destructive behavior.

Forgiving ourselves can have many benefits such as learning to love yourself in healthy ways and no longer beating yourself up for your mistakes. Life is short! If you are granted 70 years on this earth, and you've spent the last five years holding a grudge against someone, then you've spent a significant part of your life wasting time. Don't give another person power over you. Put out of your life all these things:

bad feelings about yourself and others. Refuse to carry bitter feelings. Forgive other people just as the Creator of the universe forgave you. Never pay back someone for the bad they have done. Let God take care of the situation. The One who gives you air to breathe says, "Vengeance is mine."

If the one who hates you is hungry, feed him. If he is thirsty, give him water. If you do that, you will remain in right standing with God. Do not let wrong doings have power over you. Let good have power over evil!

~

Dr. Everett Worthington, a psychologist who has researched forgiveness for decades, has developed a five-step process called Reach: R is for recall the events and the hurt as truthfully as you can. E is for Empathize. Try to understand what happened from the person who wronged you. A is for the Altruistic gift of forgiveness. Recall a time that you hurt someone else and were forgiven and offer this gift to the person who wronged you. C is for committing yourself to forgive publicly.

Write a letter of forgiveness (whether you send it or not). Write in a journal, tell a trusted friend, or, if you can, tell the person who wronged you. H is for holding onto unforgiveness. Forgiving is not forgetting. Memories of wrong and the feelings associated will surface. Remind yourself that you have made a choice to forgive.

Have you known people who are tied up in their knots of bitterness, un-forgiveness, and plots for revenge? How did they get to be that way? Un-forgiveness sits like a burden on your back. Even though the offense may be long gone, it can continue to weigh you down. When left unattended un-forgiveness can pile up, it begins to affect everything you do and everyone around you. The debris of rotting regret, shame, and anger poison the air, causing difficulties in your relationships with God, your work in the ministry and your peace of mind. Life sometimes has a way of unloading its junk on us, however; we don't have to accept it, and we don't have to carry it. If Satan can convince you to focus on your past, he can keep you from fulfilling all you were created to be. The enemy will define you by your past to confine you. Resist him. Learn from yesterday but don't live in it.

Don't look a life through the rearview mirror... Look through the windshield. For many of us, tomorrow never comes because we are tied to our past. We're carrying so much baggage from yesterday; we can't even get through today, let alone step into our future. To experience victory through forgiveness, make sure to treat your wounds. Let them heal, and rather than focusing on the scars of your past, focus on your new start. It's a new day. Live in forgiveness today, not the pain of yesterday, and step-by-step, you will move into a victorious tomorrow. You have what it takes to move forward.

Your future can be brighter than your past if you do your part. Keep in mind that forgiveness is a decision and not an emotion. It's not about how you feel, but rather about your choice to no longer let your emotions rule you.

Real-to-Real

Name the relationship, the feelings and the reasons why you need to cut the strings and let it go.

- Who: Relationship
- What: Feelings
- Why: Reason

CHAPTER 8

My Praise is Personal

Psalm 86:12-13 says, *"I will praise thee, O Lord my God, with all my heart: and I will glorify thy name forevermore. For great is thy mercy toward me: and thou hast delivered my soul from the lowest hell."* Considering all that the Lord has done for us through His Son Jesus, we have a right to praise Him.

We can praise the Lord because we have been redeemed by the blood of Jesus and are no longer in bondage by the weight of sin.

"But God demonstrates his own love for us in this: While we were still sinners, Christ died for us." (Romans 5:8).

It only takes a moment to think about how good God has been and all that He has done in our lives. When we've been low in spirit, He's been the one who picked us up and turned our sadness into joy. There's no greater joy than what the Lord so freely lavishes on us. His love never fails, and we are renewed by His power each day. There's no one like Him in all the earth; it is the Lord who comes to our rescue, restores our soul and turns our midnight into day.

The Lord is wonderful, mighty, marvelous and magnificent. With our mouth, we can shout Hallelujah to the King of kings, Hallelujah to the Lord of lords, Hallelujah to the Lord who reigns forever and ever. Let the sound of your praise echo within the walls of your home. Let the sound of your praise be released in your prayer room, in your car or wherever the Spirit of the Lord comes upon you. You have a right to praise the Lord. Praise Him in and through the *storm!*

I could hear the strong winds blow on that Saturday morning in mid-January as the great Northeastern *storm* hit the state of New Jersey and the surrounding areas. The fifty mile an hour winds were fierce. The effects of the winds blew out electricity, canceled public transportation and stalled the entire city. As I stood on my patio looking out the window and listening to the winds, I thought of the many ways storms distress our lives. Like the winds of nature that touch the seasons, and circumstances affect our lives. The wind is an unseen force that shifts the atmosphere and changes the temperature. Storms come in our lives for reasons that only God knows, however; they are guided by His hand. He knows, and He cares about all that concerns us. His Word says that His eye is on the sparrow and His eyes are on us. When the fierce winds of life blow our way, we can lift our eyes to the hills because that is where our help comes from. With the aid of the Holy Spirit, we are protected and have a place of refuge in the storm. If we allow Satan to distract us with the cares of this world, he will silence our praise and prayer life. Prayer and praise invoke the presence of the Lord and transforms the atmosphere. I believe that we can build a place of prayer and worship anywhere.

Psalms 34:1 says, *"I will extol the LORD at all times; his praise will always be on my lips."*

The flawed and the fallen, the weak and the strong, the sick and the well, can pray and lift a sound of praise to God. And as we wait on the Lord in our time with Him, surely, He will bask in the presence of our praise. God is our rock and our defense, and we are safe in His shelter.

Psalms 62:5 says, *"My soul, wait thou only upon God; for my expectation is from him."*

The loving-kindness, grace, and mercies of the Lord are our foundation, and that is the reason for our lips to forever praise Him. The Lord is our God, and our heart must be turned towards Him continuously.

When the unemployment lines were long, the Lord opened a door, and I walked in. He's worthy of my praise. When I think of the many times, I sat on the operating table, and God brought me through I can't help but praise Him. When I couldn't speak the Lord opened my mouth so that I could bring forth praise to His name and tell of the wondrous things He had done. When a battle was raging in me, I called upon the name of the Lord, and He heard me.

Psalms 55:18 says, *"He rescues me unharmed from the battle waged against me, even though many oppose me."*

Our weeping makes our praise personal. Your tears speak to God and He will answer in the time of need.

"Weeping may endure for the night, but joy cometh in the morning." (Psalms 30:5).

There were times when all I could do was moan or sigh, but God understood all of it. He is praise worthy and I'll give Him the praise that is due His name. After His crucifixion Mary Magdalene stood outside the sepulcher weeping. As she cried from the depth of her soul, Jesus appeared to her.

Jesus said to her Mary, "Woman, why weepest thou?"

And so, I ask you, why are you crying, or what has broken your spirit? The Savior of the world, the Creator of every living thing, is our Father, our refuge, our healer, and our help.

Love Lifted Me

I was sinking deep in sin
Far from the peaceful shores,
Very deeply stained within
Sinking to rise no more,
But the master of the sea
Heard my dispersing cry
And from the waters lifted me
Now Oh how safe am I.

Love lifted me and His love is available to raise anyone who needs a touch from the Master.

Psalms 23 says, *"He leadeth me beside the still waters. He restoreth my soul: he leadeth me in the paths of righteousness for his name's sake. Yea, though I walk through the valley of the shadow of death, I will fear no evil: for thou art with me; thy rod and thy staff they comfort me. Thou preparest a table before me in the presence of mine enemies: thou anoints my head with oil; my cup runneth over. Surely goodness and mercy shall follow me all the days of my life: and I will dwell in the house of the LORD forever."*

We praise God for His leading, and we praise Him for restoration. Where would any of us be if the Lord had not restored our minds? Sometimes the path that I took was far from His way, but the Lord walked with me. He comforted me, and yes, He prepared a table amid my enemies. I know about His goodness. I've experienced His mercy, and I know that He'll be with me forever. That's why I praise Him, and that's why He's worthy.

When others think we should be crying, complaining and confused, won't they be surprised to find us leaping, shouting and walking in power! Don't allow your boss, co-worker, relatives, brother, sister, saints, sinners or adversary to steal your joy or peace.

John 14:27 says, "*I am leaving you with a gift- peace of mind and heart. And the peace I give isn't fragile like the peace the world gives.*"

It is Well with my Soul

So, don't be troubled or afraid.
When peace like a river attended my way…
When sorrows like sea billows roll...
Whatever my lot thou have taught me to say,
It is well, it is well, with my soul.

You can say it is well because God knows all about it. He knows, and He hears. As children of God, we are free to express our love and adoration to the Lord. Never permit your praise to be silence. Some may say, "It doesn't take all that." However; they don't know your story! The earth declares His glory, and we were made to give Him glory. Because praise is personal, we have the right to rejoice, kneel, reel to and fro and celebrate. Be free to dance before the Lord. Clap your hands and leap for joy. The many ways God demonstrated His love for us is the reason we praise Him. It is the reason we shout, cry and bow our heads in complete silence. We extend our hands to the Lord as we reach out to Him in humble spirit thanking God for things not yet received, as well as things already done.

We all have a story to tell! Our praise is personal. After all we have endured we can still rise to face another day and prepare for another storm. Maya Angelo said it like this *"And Still I Rise."* Sometimes weary but we get up, at times disappointed but rise above. There's no other way to move toward your destiny than to look up to the One who was hung high on the cross of Calvary for us and got up with all power; gave us that same power. We can reflect upon that one miracle of God and face any so-called giant that comes our way! Despite circumstances, we have the ability of the Almighty to step out on faith and watch God do just what He said, and just what He promised. *We still rise, and we increase with power and purpose.*

"Jesus said unto him, Rise, take up thy bed, and walk." (John 5:8).

If you find yourself with the condition of spiritual paralysis, the question is... *do you want to get well?*

CHAPTER 9

Temptation: Those Pearly Whites

Every day of our lives we are engaged in war. This was not of a physical nature but a spiritual one. It is a war between our spirit and our flesh. It is a war that encompasses our thought patterns. How we filter information from our past and our future. Information comes from many different sources. Perhaps, we received values, beliefs or religious practices from our parents, the church or the world's values, beliefs and religious practices. The world system is opposed to the teachings of God, and one of Satan's tricks is to keep people spiritually dead. In a world where bad seems good and good seems evil, the two mixed can result in confusion. The world's views can corrupt your mind by dumping its garbage into our thinking. The Word of God is our ammunition to counter act the attacks of Satan and his stinking thinking.

If the information in your brain is wrong, it is influencing your mind (deteriorating your conscience), which is affecting the condition of your spirit. Our heart, soul, and mind are interconnected. The man is a triune being: body, soul, and spirit. The devil's battle ground is the mind. He does not attack us in recognizable ways because if he did, we would not walk in his plan. He will try to trick us into believing that our thoughts line up with the Word of God; so that our behavior is contrary to the will of the Father. Later he will influence us to justify our actions. When and if his plan is fulfilled we realize that he has deceived us and we must turn to God. Throughout this chapter, we will look at how our thoughts affect our decisions and what is the role of the mind, heart, and soul.

The inspiration of God gives all Scripture. The inspired Word gives us the ability through the Holy Spirit to discern what is imparted into our subconscious. If our thoughts are resistant to the Word, a red light should go on. This means that we should dismiss the idea and align our thinking to Godly instructions. Knowledge or information is released in the mind as it was with Eve and then it was transmitted in the form of thoughts. (Read the story and pay close attention to the process of reflection).

The heart is the residence for our:
- Thoughts
- Passions
- Desires
- Appetites
- Bad way or good
- Affections
- Emotions

Faylynn's Story

Faylynn was a middle-aged and attractive Africa-America woman. She worked in corporate America for many years and enjoyed her job. Faylynn was very involved in ministry at her Church and was looking forward to fulfilling the assignment that God had entrusted to her; with surrounding Christian support groups for women and being a motivational speaking.

Faylynn would go to church on Sunday's and occasionally attend evening worship or church revivals. One Saturday after a women's breakfast at church she was greeted by her brother in Christ; James. The conversation was lengthy. After she had walked away, she said Ah, he seems very nice, and it was delightful to have a pleasant conversation with a man.

CHAPTER 10

It Seemed So Innocent

Week after week Faylynn would see James standing in the church foyer at the exit door, and there was no way she could miss his presence. There he stood each week as she passed flashing that dazzling smile as she walked by. During one of their hello's, he expressed some sadness over the death of a family member. The news saddened Faylynn, and she

97

shared her condolences. When Faylynn went home that night, she didn't do much work on her ministry assignment as she normally did each night. She found herself thinking of the brother and how she could lift his spirit. It had been years since Faylynn had been out with a man. She thought that asking him out would lift his spirits and at the time it seemed innocent. After church on the following Sunday as James was standing in his usual spot; sure to be in her view, Faylynn said hello and asked him if he'd like to go out sometime? He flashed those pearly whites and replied with an astounding, yes! At first, Faylynn thought a movie and dinner would be all right, but after a while, she decided to search for a dinner cruise.

CHAPTER 11

You Better Think…Drifting Away

Philippians 4:6-8 says, *"Be careful for nothing; but in everything by prayer and supplication with thanksgiving let your requests be made known unto God. And the peace of God, which passes all understanding, shall keep your hearts and minds through Christ Jesus."* Every cruise line she contacted was booked up, and she became frustrated. However, she was determined to make this date happen. So,

relentlessly she keeps trying until finally, she books the dinner cruise with an excellent company. She spent days looking for the perfect outfit. Faylynn was excited and wanted everything to be perfect from head to toe. She made an appointment for her hair and nails. She wore a beautiful multicolored blouse with baby blue, pink and green abstract designs that fit well with the white background. The black palazzo pants made the outfit complete. Her pedicured toes matched well with the color of her blouse, and she felt beautiful. Something she had not felt in quite some time.

Spiritual Cataracts...Impaired Vision

Proverbs 4:20-27 says, *"My son, attend to my words; incline thine ear unto my sayings. Let them not depart from thine eyes; keep them in the midst of thine heart. For they are life unto those that find them, and health to all their flesh. Keep thy heart with all diligence; for out of it are the issues of life. Put away from thee a froward mouth, and perverse lips put far from thee. Let thine eyes look right on, and let thine eyelids look straight before thee. Ponder the path of thy feet, and let all thy ways be established. Turn not to the right hand nor the left; remove thy foot from evil."*

Finally, the day arrived. The doorbell rang, and she took a deep breath and opened the door. Almost instantly she looks at his smile and admires his fully shaped lips.

He looked amazing! Six feet three inches, deep dark chocolate skin and wearing a good tailor shirt that showed his biceps and custom tailor pants. His shoes freshly polished with a luminous shine that caught her attention; he looked fine, to say the least.

"For the cravings of the lower nature are opposed to those of the spirit, and the cravings of the spirit are opposed to those of the low nature; because these are antagonistic to each other so that you cannot do everything to which you are inclined." (Galatians 5:17).

He opened the car door and helped her in, and they began to talk. She did most of the talking, but he was able to chime in on occasion. It was a beautiful summer evening. The drive to the pier was about one hour, and as they approached the cruise line, they could smell the ocean water. The temperature was about 70 degrees and the sun would be setting shortly. When they entered the cruise line, the waitress escorted them to their table. The table was on the side of the waterfront and the view of the ocean was spectacular. The dinner menu was delicious and Faylynn ever ordered an alcoholic drink. The music was from their era even though he was ten years older than she. After dinner, James asked if she'd like to go out and take a seat on the outer deck. She said yes!

The skies were very clear and luminous on that beautiful summer night, and the moon appeared to have a smile on its face.

CHAPTER 12

Warning Signs...Proceed with Caution

Just as traffic lights control the movement of vehicles in relationships we are given signs that tell us to stop, proceed with caution or go. We must yield to the right of way, and that good way is the way that the Word has mapped out for our lives. There are always warning signs when things are not right in a relationship and do not fit into the plan that God has for your life. Do you notice the warning signs? What do you do? Acknowledge them or pretend they don't exists. When you're not sure what to do, yield your will and desires to God. Stop immediately and let the Lord show you the unseen. Love on the expressway can end up on a dead end.

If you're not in Love with the One who loves you most then you're not in love at all.

~

He stood behind her as they both looked out at the ocean. His body was pressed against hers and she felt that it was too close, but it felt good so she didn't say anything.

"Watch and pray so that you will not fall into temptation. The spirit is willing, but the flesh is weak." (Matthew 26:41).

CHAPTER 13

Love on the Expressway…Ended on a Dead End

Then slowly she turned around wanting to step back but instead he pulled her closer, and it happened. He first kissed her gently and then very passionately. It was the beginning of an affair that ended in depression, guilt, shame, rejection, and repentance. Love on the expressway terminated on an impasse. Faylynn's dead end relationship with James was the path that lead her to a love relationship with Christ. Faylynn's way of thinking about love, life and relationships were transformed as she sought God through prayer.

We will experience love in many ways as it is demonstrated by others. However; the only unconditional love (Agape) that will last throughout eternity is the love of God through Jesus Christ.

"Finally, my brethren, be strong in the Lord, and in the power of his might. Wherefore take unto you the whole armor of God that ye may be able to withstand in the evil day, and having done all, to stand. Stand therefore, having your loins girt about with truth, and having on the breastplate of righteousness; and your feet shod with the preparation of the gospel of peace. Above all, taking the shield of faith, wherewith ye shall be able to quench all the fiery darts of the wicked. And take the helmet of salvation, and the sword of the Spirit, which is the Word of God." (Ephesians 6:10, 13-17).

The only way to live a victorious Christian life is to be continually mindful of God's mercy, grace, faithfulness, goodness, love, and kindness. God will give us peace of mind if we continue to trust in Him. No circumstance will defeat us nor even discourage us if we trust in the Lord God Almighty.

When we are being led by the Spirit, we will have our minds set on the things of the Spirit and on living a life that is

106

pleasing to the Lord and doing His will. When we are led by our flesh, we will have our minds set on the desires of our flesh. Our flesh has no desire to please God. King David was said to be a man after God's own heart. Yet, he beheld a beautiful woman who was not his and desired her.

"It happened, late one afternoon, when David arose from his couch and was walking on the roof of the king's house, that he saw from the roof a woman bathing; and the woman was gorgeous. David sent and inquired about the woman. And one said, "Is not this Bathsheba, the daughter of Elian, the wife of Uriah the Hittite?" (2 Samuel 11:3).

David committed adultery, conspiracy to commit murder, and then premeditated murder. David was not where he should have been during the time of battle in the land. When David first saw Bathsheba, he should have a looked away. Even when David found out that she was married, he proceeded with his plans. Uriah, Bathsheba's husband, was killed at David's command.

Even the men and women of faith in the Bible fell short. We see how God dealt with sin and mistakes. God forgives, however; we must acknowledge our faults and fall on our knees before Him to repent to be restored. Jesus was innocent, yet; he died for the guilty. Every day in our lives we are given the right to choose. We choose who we will let into our space. We choose how we will interrupt words and choose what to believe. As it was with Eve in the garden, so it is with all of us. We must make our choices based on the Word of God and the guidance of the Holy Spirit.

In Genesis, we read of the dialog between the serpent and Eve. *"Now the serpent was more crafty than any of the wild animals the LORD God had made. He said to the woman, "Did God really say, 'You must not eat from any tree in the garden'?"* (Genesis 3:1).

The result of conversation had a drastic consequence on the entire world and the relationship between God and man. Eve was knowledgeable of God's command, however; she made a choice to listen and have dialog with the serpent. Eve senses were drawn to the voice of Satan. She heard with her ears, looked with her eyes and tasted with her mouth. What we allow to enter our ear gate goes into our spirit and can either help us or hinder us. We must filter our conversation and only allow that which is edifying for our spirits to enter in. We should be watching and praying always.

"Keep thy heart with all diligence; for out of it are the issues of life." (Proverbs 4:23).

In the heat of the moment, things can quickly get out of control. Lust and love are very different. Love is patient: lasciviousness requires immediate satisfaction. Love is kind; lust is harsh. Love does not demand its way; lust does. When any one of the five senses awaken through physical stimulation, a biological change can occur in a matter of seconds.

Much of the pain and tragedy in relationships is avoidable if people would be honest with themselves and with each other. Instead, they hide their faults and mislead the other into thinking they are someone they are not.

• Heart/Mind:

"For the word of God is quick, and powerful, and sharper than any two-edged sword, piercing even to the dividing asunder of soul and spirit, and of the joints and marrow, and is a discerner of the thoughts and intents of the heart." (Hebrews 4:12).

• Eye/See:

"The precepts of the Lord are right, giving joy to the heart. The commands of the Lord are radiant, giving light to the eyes." (Psalm 19:8).

• Ear/Hear:

"For the ear tests words as the tongue tastes food." (Job 34:3).

• Mouth/Speak:

"Whoso keepeth his mouth and his tongue keepeth his soul from troubles." (Proverbs 21:23).

• Hand/Touch:

"A man will be satisfied with good by the fruit of his words, And the deeds of a man's hands will return to him." (Proverbs 12:14).

• Feet/Direction:

"Trust in the Lord with all thine heart: and lean not unto thine own understanding, in all thy ways acknowledge him, and He shall direct thy paths." (Proverbs 3:5-6).

"Teach me your way, O LORD, and I will walk in your truth; give me an undivided heart, that I may fear your name." (Psalm 86:11).

"I the LORD search the heart and examine the mind, to reward a man according to his conduct, according to what his deeds deserve." (Jeremiah 17:10).

"But the things that come out of the mouth come from the heart," (Matthew 15:18).

CHAPTER 14

Seducing Spirits: Temptations, Desires, and Decisions

Fleshly desires will lead one into the areas of disobedience or disloyalty by persuasion or false promises. Seducing spirits will led those that follow astray. Being astray is somewhat like roaming, wandering or being lost. Lust will corrupt our thinking and entice us to partake of something that is unhealthy. When we are tempted there is a sincere desire to possess whatever the craving might be. Seduction will promote enslavement or overpower us. We know that Satan is called *"The Tempter."* When Satan tempts us, he uses the evil desires that are in our flesh as a vehicle. He merely dangles the bait, and if we're not careful, we can be overtaken.

Our flesh is hungry for sin. Our flesh knows nothing but sin and desires nothing but sin.

Paul put it this way, *"Nothing good lives in me, that is, in my sinful nature (flesh)."* (Romans 7:18).

Sin separates us from God, and when we're separated from God, we are susceptible to the toxicity of this world.

Real-to-Real

- What intrigued Faylynn about her new acquaintance?
- Where Faylynn's intentions good?
- Why do you suppose Faylynn became distracted in her ministry assignment?
- Why did Faylynn become frustrated when her plans were difficult to arrange?
- What didn't Faylynn do before asking him?
- Why was Faylynn so concerned about her outfit,

clothes, and hair?

- What was the first thing Faylynn's noticed when she opened the door?
- What do you think his reasons were for asking to go on deck? Did he have a motive?
- Should Faylynn have changed her standing position?
- Why didn't she?
- Was Faylynn deceived?

CHAPTER 15

Her Story: It Seemed So Innocent

His eyes shined like the warmth of the summer sunlight. His voice was soft yet masculine and his Southern drawl was appealing. When he looked at her; her entire mind and body went on shutdown. He was a working man and a lavish spender. He always purchased nice things for her. Jewelry, shoes, designer bags, you name it nothing she asked for was denied. He always paid for dinner, and they went to the theater often. Theater tickets would often cost over two-hundred dollars, but the price was not an issue with him. He frequently made comments about his love for God and how the Lord had delivered him from a rough life. He was a faithful worker in the church and held multiple positions. Everyone who knew him loved him, and he was a man who could be counted on. He appeared to have it all.

She, on the other hand, was not involved in church ministries. She went to church on Sunday's to hear the Word, however; she never went to Sunday school or mid-week Bible study. She was on a fixed income and was happy with going to work each day and coming home to a hot bubble bath, dinner and watching her pre-recorded soap operas. As time went by she fell in love with the lifestyle he offered her. It felt great to have someone pay for everything and treat her like a queen. The attention was enjoyable, and she began to feel that her life had a purpose.

The more time they spent together, the more attracted they became to each other. In the beginning, she would pray before they would eat dinner at the restaurant. At the end of their evening she would pray again. As time went on long passionate kisses sealed the nights replacing unsaid prayers. The kisses included the firm yet gentle rubbing of the strong hands she had grown to admire. With each kiss and each touch of his hands, they both slowly slipped away into ecstasy. Passion had replaced praise and worship… drifting away with each touch.

~

Desire may be accomplished when one walks in the flesh, but lasting relationships may not always be the result. The scripture says that there is no good thing in the flesh. Therefore, we cannot be ruled by it. If we allow our minds to be dominated by our flesh our life will be empty, without purpose, and not be pleasing to God. Being heavenly minded pleases God.

Romans 8:6-10 says, *"Seek ye first the kingdom of heaven and all things shall be added unto you. For to be carnally minded is death, but to be spiritually minded is life and peace. Because the carnal mind is enmity against God: for it is not subject to the law of God, neither indeed can be. So then they that are in the flesh cannot please God. But ye are not in the flesh, but in the Spirit, if so be that the Spirit of God dwells in you. Now if any man has not the Spirit of Christ, he is none of his. And if Christ is in you, the body is dead because of sin; but the Spirit is life because of righteousness."*

The greatest of all God's commandments for us is that we love Him with all our beings, and that cannot be accomplished unless we keep our minds on Him.

117

Matthew 22:37-38 says, "*Jesus said unto him, thou shalt love the Lord thy God with all thy heart, and with all thy soul, and with all thy mind. This is the first and great commandment.*"

Our thoughts are the genesis to our actions. Our actions generate our reality. Our reality determines our destiny and Christ consciousness should always be at the forefront. As a Believer in Christ, we are not of this world, and we don't pattern our thinking like those of the world. Our minds are being renewed daily by God's power working in us. We are different, and our desire is to please God our Father. Like the wick of a candle burns minutes after the fire is blown out; it only takes one flick of a match to restart the flame. So, it is with us. Sometimes our spiritual light grows dim, and we don't detect problem areas in our lives until the consequence of our actions begin to affect us.

Our reasoning can become clouded in the heat of the moment. Maybe our prayer and fasting life is lacking and if these areas in our lives are untreated the symptoms with eventually show up. We cannot afford to be impaired or blinded by Satan's devices. The lady in the story can start over again. All it takes is one touch from the Master. If we humble ourselves before Him, repent of our sins, He is faithful to forgive.

Real-to-Real

When we fail to apply what has been sown into our lives through the preached or taught Word; what are the results? The sayings are old but they still hold true. You can't tell a book by its cover, and everything that glitters isn't gold! What does the story say about his prayer life? Why is it important to practice what you preach? Our completeness must be found in our relationship with Christ. Our lives have a God-given purpose and we must seek God to find it. Why is repentance important? Why did the lady in the story lose her praise and worship?

Mind Changer

"No temptation has overtaken you except what is common to mankind. And God is faithful; he will not let you be tempted beyond what you can bear. But when you are tempted, he will also provide a way out so that you can endure it." (1 Corinthians 10:13).

CHAPTER 16

Dreamann's Story

Proverbs 3:16, *"In all thy ways acknowledge him, and he shall direct thy paths."* Isaiah 30:12, *"And thine ears shall hear a word behind thee, saying, this is the way, walk ye in it, when ye turn to right hand, and when ye turn to the left."*

Dreamanna was in her early forties and twice divorced. Even after two failed marriages she still wanted to be married again. She wanted to be wanted by someone who would accept her as she was and never leave her alone. She wanted a home, a place filled with life, memories and a gentle kiss at the end of the day. She wanted security. Dreamanna was consumed with loneliness as she walked into her one-bedroom apartment each day with no one to greet her. Each night she would clutch a cold pillow. She had no one to go out to dinner with or take in a movie. Dreamanna was alone in a world filled with so many people. One evening while talking with a friend, she was introduced to an online Christian dating website. After viewing the dating site, Dreamanna decided to register. Instantly she wrote a profile about herself attached an old picture and began her search. When Dreamanna began to list the criteria for the man of her dreams she began to smile. Wow, she said, "*I'll select everything I want in the man for me that I like*… Height 6 feet, weighs 250 pounds, eyes, light brown, hair salt and pepper age, 45-60, should be financially stable, religion: Baptist or Pentecostal, *open*." She wanted him to be educated, working and not demanding. She wanted to go out for dinner at least twice a week, enjoy vacations together and buy her nice things. Dreamanna felt like she was on the right track with this Christian dating service.

In a brief prayer, she said: "God you can use any method to bring people together, if it is your will, *please send me a husband!*" Once Dreamanna hit *send* the site responded immediately with the type of men she was looking for. Day-after-day Dreamanna would spend countless hours reading profiles and responding. Finally, there was a decisive match. After numerous email correspondences, both parties decided to share their phone numbers. When Dreamanna came home from work one evening the incoming light on her phone was blinking. As soon as Dreamanna heard the voicemail message her heart leaped for joy.

"Hello, Dreamanna this is Darious. Your voice sounds so sweet I can't wait to talk with you. Please give me a call."

For almost one-year Darious called Dreamanna virtually every night. He promised her that he would visit her, but something would always come up. He talked about the gifts he purchased for her, but somehow, they never arrived in the mail.

Finally, after living with a broken promise of meeting him in person for over 11 months, things were looking bright. Darious said he had made an airline reservation and would be arriving on Airway Express Flight 007 at 12:01 A.M. on Thursday, July 22nd. The night before Dreamanna called Darious to confirm their meeting; his phone rang and rang until it finally diverted to voicemail. Darious never arrived, and she never heard from him.

Dreamanna was a 'I' want it like this and 'I' want it like that kinda woman. Being idle and lonely is an open invitation for the voice of the enemy to creep in a fill your spirit with worldliness.

The grandest space we can ever occupy is a place of pure contentment found deep within each of us. Tapping into our inner selves-our willingness to love, commitment to goals, dedication and compassion for others-gives us entrance to the most majestic house ever built; the one that houses the soul. Take your own 'house tour' and discover the palace within you.

"If a man happens to find himself, he has a mansion which he can inhabit with dignity all the days of his life." (James A. Michener).

CHAPTER 17

When A Man Loves a Woman…A Look at Love

John 3:16-17, *"For God so loved the world, that he gave his only begotten Son, that whosoever believeth in him should not perish, but have everlasting life. For God sent not his Son into the world to condemn the world; but that the world through him might be saved."* Mark 12:30-31, *"And thou shalt love the Lord thy God with all thy heart, and with all thy soul, and with thy entire mind, and with all thy strength: this is the*

first commandment. And the second is like, namely this, thou shalt love thy neighbor as thyself. There is none other commandment greater than these."

Love, a four-letter word can flow from the lips like butter in a hot skillet and water from a fountain, and warm the heart of the hearer like no other word in the dictionary. Love according to Merriam Webster Dictionary can be defined as having a deep attraction, affection or emotional attachment to a person, people or thing. But what is love? Individuals define love differently, what may be love to one person may not mean the same to another. Many of us show love in the ways we hope to receive love, but it does not always happen that way.

1 Corinthians 13:4-8a says, *"Love suffers long and is kind; love does not envy; love does not parade itself, is not puffed up; does not behave rudely, does not seek its own, is not provoked, thinks no evil; does not rejoice in iniquity, but rejoices in the truth; bears all things, believes all things, hopes all things, endures all things. Love never fails."*

In today's world, it appears the word love is used so freely, so casual yet; the depth of its meaning somehow gets lost when uttered without real worth and action.

Her Story:

11:00 A.M Worship Service

His brass baritone voice rang throughout the sanctuary on that summer Sunday morning during worship service as he sang *Jesus Is the Light of the World*. The atmosphere was high and the presence of the Lord was in the house. The musicians were all in tune with the sounds blazing from each instrument. The congregation was filled with songs of praise, the lifting of hands and the shouts of Hallelujah sprang forth as that of a trumpet. Unfortunately, the dark veil of the night before silenced my praise. How could I sing about the light of the world when lust lurked in my flesh?

Romans 6:12-13 says, *"Let not sin therefore reign in your mortal body, that ye should obey it in the lusts thereof. Neither yield ye your members as instruments of unrighteousness unto sin: but yield yourselves unto God, as those that are alive from the dead, and your members as instruments of righteousness unto God."*

"Love is something eternal-the aspect may change, but not the essence." (Vincent Van Gogh).

Although true love lasts forever, over time its aspect alters: The intensity of new love or new friendship eventually matures into an enduring, comfortable relationship. When you

127

find yourself moving beyond the blush of new love, remember that if your love is real, it will transcend all of life's unalterable through time.

"But God demonstrates his own love for us in this: While we were still sinners, Christ died for us." (Romans 5:8).

God did demonstrate His love for us in giving His Son to die once for all in the past for our sins. But He also knows that this past love must be experienced as a present reality (today and tomorrow) if we are to have patience and character and hope.

It's useless to expect from man what can only come from the Divine. When a man loves a woman, his ears and heart should be attuned and attentive to her voice.

Her Story – Preach!

His clergy robe dazzled with colors of black and gold and his presence spoke power even with words unspoken. The resurrection message was *Out of the Grave He Arose*. There buried beneath the weight of guilt and shame was a woman who genuinely loved the Lord. How could a woman who was desolate and lived in a dark and dreary place find the Divine who brought deliverance and awakened destiny?

The message of the cross is this *God saves the lost, lifts the fallen and heals the wounded.* The God kind of love flows from the pulpit to the pew. All of us are sinners; saved by grace. Grace is the unmerited favor of God showering upon us. Love is demonstrated in our lives when we "Love" a person enough not to lead them into a situation that would hinder their walk with the Lord.

"He made Him who knew no sin to be sin on our behalf that we might become the righteousness of God in Him." (2 Corinthians 5:21).

"But God, being rich in mercy, because of the great love with which he loved us, even when we were dead in our trespasses, made us alive together with Christ; by grace, you have been saved." (Ephesians 2:4-5).

CHAPTER 18

Conditions of the Heart

Proverbs 4:23, *"Keep thy heart with all diligence; for out of it are the issues of life."* The heart is the root component of choice. My spirit broke, and the weights of responsibilities were heavy. I felt all hope was gone. I froze in time, and my future seemed bleak. The voices within lead me to the refrigerator, and the mall; neither could satisfy the emptiness I felt inside. The bouts

with panic attacks would come at any given moment throughout the day but mostly at night. During the evening when I wanted to sleep, I found myself jumping out of bed and running to the front door gasping for air. I wanted to escape the feeling of being shackled, bound by the reality of my current situation. My escape to the evening air gave me a moment of tranquility, so I thought.

The prescribed medications called my name throughout the night. Prozac, Xanax, Zoloft, and Wellbutrin beckoned my attention without fail. I surrendered to the seduction of prescribed drugs like an addict on cocaine craving an immediate fix. One night, I jumped out of bed and ran to the door for air as I often did. In a severe manic episode, I then ran back to my bedroom and reached for my prescription. As I began to lift the cap off the medicine bottle, a voice from within called me to remember the God who heals. I put the cap back on the pill bottle and placed it in the drawer. You may ask "what happened?" I decided to put my cares in the hands of the Master. I touched God through faith, and He took the broken pieces of my life and renewed my inner being.

As you *navigate through the seasons of your life* trust God for spiritual and physical healing. God is able, and in Him, we take hold of the abundant life.

He Touched Me

He touched me
Shackled by a heavy burden
'Neath a load of guilt and shame
Then the hand of Jesus touched me

And now I am no longer the same
For He touched me, oh He touched me
And oh what a joy that floods my soul
Something happened and now I know

He touched me and made me whole
Oh since I met this blessed Savior
And since he cleaned and made me whole
Oh I never cease, never cease to praise Him

I'll shout it while eternity rolls
Oh He touched me, oh He touched me
And oh what a joy that floods my soul
Something happened and now I know
He touched me and made me whole
(William J. Gaither).

CHAPTER 19

Release Your Spiritual Essence: You Are Valuable

Matthew 5:14, *"You are the light of the world. A town built on a hill cannot be hidden."* How much worth do you put on your life? I'm not talking about dollars and cents. Sometimes we confuse our self-worth by the things we possess, houses, land, money, cars, college degrees and other tangible things. However; your value has little to do with your valuables. You

are priceless. You count to God. You are valuable. God loves us so much that He gave His only Son for us.

"For God so loved the world that he gave his only begotten Son, that whosoever believeth in him should not perish, but have everlasting life." (John 3:16).

Additionally, according to Ephesians 2:10, *"For we are his workmanship, created in Christ Jesus unto good works, which God hath before ordained that we should walk in them."* We are so valuable to God that he says, *nothing can separate us from His love.*

Mind Changer

"Who shall separate us from the love of Christ? Shall tribulation, or distress, or persecution, or famine, or nakedness, or peril, or sword? As it is written, for thy sake we are killed all the day long; we are accounted as sheep for the slaughter, Nay, in all these things we are more than conquerors through him that loved us. For I am persuaded, that neither death, nor life, nor angels, nor principalities, nor powers, nor things present, nor things to come, nor height, nor depth, nor any other creature, shall be able to separate us from the love of God, which is in Christ Jesus our Lord." (Romans 8:35-39).

- There was the woman with the issue of blood
- The woman who was bent over
- The woman at the well
- The blind man
- Jesus fed 5000

1 Corinthians 12:15-26 says, *"If the foot shall say because I am not the hand, I am not of the body; is it therefore not of the body? And if the ear shall say because I am not the eye, I am not of the body; is it therefore not of the body? If the whole body were an eye, where were the hearing? If the whole were hearing, where were the smelling? But now hath God set the members every one of them in the body, as it hath pleased him. And if they were all one member, where were the body? But now are they many members, yet but one body.*

And the eye cannot say unto the hand, I have no need of thee: nor again the head to the feet, I have no need of you. Nay, much more those members of the body, which seem to be more feeble, are necessary. And those members of the body, which we think to be less honorable, upon these we bestow more abundant honor; and our uncomely parts have more abundant comeliness. For our comely parts have no need: but God hath tempered the body together, having given more abundant honor to that part which lacked. That there should be no schism in the body; but that the members should have the same care one for another. And whether one member suffers, all the members suffer with it; or one member is honored, all the members rejoice with it. How much Jesus loves us!"

137

Think about how Jesus, the great mighty Creator, became a man and walked among us, and then was crucified in the hands of those He had created. He did it because He loved and valued us so much, that He wanted to save us from our sins. The worth of a human soul can be estimated only by the light reflected from the cross of Calvary.

Has the following question ever crossed your mind? How do I get to a place in my life when I can feel that I'm on top of the world and not at rock bottom or somewhere in between? Is there a place that makes me feel that I am somebody, I do belong, and I can achieve extra ordinary things? I know I have potential, and at times I could take the world on all by myself.

So, why are there times when I feel stabilized in my life, not going anywhere, fighting the same battles and going around the same mountain? How do I get out of the nest of despair and sail beyond my difficult circumstances? One day I'll be able to say, "*mountain move out of my way*" and Satan get thee behind me.

One morning as I walked to my car, I noticed a small bird sitting on the hood, to get it off I waved my hands and shouted shoo, shoo. With no avail, I started the car and pulled off, being confident that once I got on route in the fast-moving traffic the little bird would surely fly away.

Well needless to say it didn't. So I pulled over at a nearby gas station. The attendant came over, scooped the bird up in his hands and gently lifted it in the air, and off the bird went. Like that little bird, there are times when we too need a gentle push to get in the place where God wants us to be. There is a place found only in God that will allow us to fly over depression, loneliness, despair and low self-esteem. There is a place found in God that will enable us to fly over the mess. We all know what mess is, don't we?

Mess: Confusion, disorder, and turmoil, jealousy, gossip, two-faced folk, you know those people that befriend you one day and act like they don't know you the next time you see them. It stinks, looks nasty and leaves a lasting odor if it's not cleaned up.

Butterfly Scripture

"Behold, I give unto you power to tread on serpents and scorpions, and over all the powers of the enemy, and nothing shall by any means hurt you." (Luke 10:19).

Did you know that 32 times in Scripture the eagle is used as an example of the Christian life? Eagles are extraordinary birds that are born to soar higher and faster than any other bird. We are God's eagles, made to fly. Eagles always build their nests in the highest possible place for three reasons:

139

- As protection from their enemies

- As a resting place for surveying the territory

- As an energy-saving launching pad

Trying to soar from the ground up will never work. Have you been flapping your wings but going nowhere? You need a better launching pad. Isaiah chapter 40 reminds us that the Word of our God stands forever and it is the place where a destination is started, desires are met and the dawning of a new day begins. The Word of God is our nesting place. It is our place of protection from the attacks of the enemy and a place where we can be nourished. Varying situations in life require us to walk on, walk over, walk through and walk out on our journey through *the seasons of life.*

- Walk on: to take advantage of.

- Walk over: to treat disapprovingly.

- Walk through: to go through.

- Leave: to leave suddenly; abandon, desert, forsake (means to leave without intending to return).

"Though I walk in the midst of trouble, thou wilt revive me: thou shalt stretch forth thine hand against the wrath of mine enemies, and thy right hand shall save me." (Psalms 13:7).

On our life's journey, we will encounter many things. On the cloudy days, we must let the light of God's Word guide us. When the storms of life are raging, we must trust in the Lord with all our heart. We must remember that His eye is on the sparrow and know that He watches over us. I used to think that I could not go on and life was nothing but an awful song. Now I know the meaning of true love and I am leaning on the everlasting arms of the Lord, who created us to *soar!*

SOAR: To ascend to a higher or more exalted level. Your body must be equipped with the necessary muscles to fly. What are the intrinsic spiritual muscles needed to fly? To survive, eagles depend on their ability to travel. Their bodies are designed for flight. To be a good flyer, an eagles' body must be both robust and lightweight. To be lightweight means that you are not carrying around things that can hold you down. As we feed on the Word of God, we become strong. In my research on the eagle, it says that most of the lift that powers the eagle into the air comes from the downward stroke. Because the downward stroke is so important, the muscles responsible for this motion are huge.

If I'm to be empowered, I must be in the downward position, which is prayer, as I kneel in prayer I get up in power to soar above my circumstances, beyond my inabilities, beyond my despair, beyond the strongholds of the enemy. *Prayer makes*

141

us strong for the flight of life. We are on a journey, and our destination is ultimately heaven.

People will disappoint you; circumstance will go sour; your dreams may crumble, and your hopes may be dashed. But I can absolutely, positively guarantee you that Jesus will never fail you. If you fly straight into the arms of Jesus, you will have victory over your enemies, and you'll soar on wings of an eagle.

Exodus 19:4 says, *"Ye have seen what I did unto the Egyptians, and how I bared you on eagle's wings and brought you unto myself."*

Releasing our spiritual essence means that we've decided to die to self. We've made a change from the inside out. It is no longer about us, but Christ who lives in us. The essence of who He is has become who we are. In the garden of Gethsemane, Jesus said, *"Not my will, but thy will be done."* Jesus submitted to the Father; and when we submit to Him, it makes it easier to be led by those in authority over us. Saying yes to the Lord means you may have to leave some friends, you may have to let go of some things you hold dear, you may be lonely and want to cry. However, there must be a breaking in the spirit that moves us beyond where we are to the best of what God has for us. We are in fact in the Potter's hands.

If you let go and let God *navigate you through the seasons of life,* He'll lead you to your divine assignment. He'll do things in your life that you never imagined. Our Creator opens doors that no man can shut! He'll restore your self-confidence, and if you're single, you'll find out what it means to be content in your singleness. *Renewing Your Mind & Transforming Your Life* is all about what God can do in a surrendered life. There are four things that people do in your life:

- Add
- Subtract
- Divide
- Multiply

When you release your spiritual essence, it will add power to the lives of others. Your essence will not divide people but will increase in love.

"Those who look to him are radiant; their faces are never covered with shame." (Psalms 34:5).

Many influential artists painted famous masterpieces, however; none compare to the frame and design that God created when He made you in His image.

Let the music inside of you be heard by those around you. Your song is your life's story. The beauty of who you are is yearning to be released. Don't look around you, look within because that is the place where treasures are found. As women, we are priceless jewels. The value of our distinctive quality is

143

high. Like rubies women symbolize love passion, strength and wisdom. We are the sapphires spread throughout Africa and we long for peace and contentment.

Worthy

- **W**ork on eliminating negative attitudes and beliefs.
- **O**btain a scriptural understanding of having love for yourself.
- **R**efuse to compare yourself with others.
- **T**hank God for His unconditional love for you.
- **H**ope in God's promises to complete the work He has begun in your life.
- **Y**ield your talents and abilities to helping others and see God bless your life.

CHAPTER 20

Celebrate…Embracing Your Distinctiveness

Genesis 1:26a, *"Then God said, "Let Us (Father, Son, Holy Spirit) make man in Our image, according to Our likeness [not physical, but a spiritual personality and moral likeness];"* Genesis 2:22, *"And the rib which the Lord God had taken from the man He made (fashioned, formed) into a woman, and He brought her and presented her to the man.* (AMP). Her color is not limited to the blackness of

the night, for she comes in many different shades, many different styles she is unique.

Beautiful

She was beautiful,

but not like those girls in the magazine.

She was beautiful, for the way she thought.

She was beautiful for the sparkle in her eyes

when she talked about something she loved.

She was beautiful for her ability

to make other people smile

even if she was sad.

No, she wasn't beautiful

for something as temporary as her looks.

She was beautiful deep down to her soul.

(F. Scott Fitzgerald).

'The Christian always has reason to celebrate. When we fail, celebrate His grace. When we are blessed, celebrate His mercy. When others reject us, celebrate His Love.' (Larry Crabb).

There is only one person that can give true definition to women, and that is God. God is the Creator of woman and the Architect of her existence. The essence of women can be found in the pages of the *Old and New Testament* readings, and it can be found in the lives of every woman. Within the pages of the inspired Word: you can unveil women who press their way to receive a touch from the Lord, women who suffered from an identity crisis, women who were possessed with demons and women that were used by God to do great things for the cause of Christ.

The beauty of a woman does not lie in her fancy outfits or flawless makeup. A woman's beauty lies within. Within her are strength, courage, joy, peace, and love. The power of a woman lies in her determination to meet every obstacle, weather the storms of life, bridge gaps, give life, worship and praise God.

Look within for a real glimpse of who you are and what you were created to do, trusting the Holy Spirit to lead you on the journey of life. Life is a journey of grace to live of our own free will. You were made in the image of God, and your life has a purpose. With the *natural mind*, none of us can tell what our possibilities are. Our ways are not like God's.

Our Heavenly Father knows what assignments we can handle and what spiritual gifts He has given us to accomplish His will. When you seek God with your whole heart, you will find Him. When you search for and develop a relationship with the Father, He will show you great and mighty things.

Nehemiah 2:20 says, *"We are servants of the God who rules from heaven, and he will make our work succeed, so we will start rebuilding."*

Each of us received the call from Jesus to go into the entire world. There is a place for you in Kingdom building. Always remember that *you can do all things through Christ who gives you the strength.* (Philippians 4:19). When you begin the journey of reaching the lost and strengthening the body of Christ, you will discover that there is no greater work, no greater goal *than to pursue the things of God.*

Celebrate and resolve to be Happy

To get up each morning with the resolve to be happy is to set our own conditions to the events of each day. To do this is to condition circumstances instead of being conditioned by them.

Celebrate-Troubles are Experiences

If you will call your troubles experiences, and remember that every experience develops some latent force within you, you will grow vigorous and happy, however adverse your circumstances may seem to be. You can never cross the ocean unless you have the courage to lose sight of the shore.

Celebrate Quiet Courage

Courage doesn't always roar. Sometimes courage is the quiet voice at the end of the day saying, *'I will try again tomorrow.'*

Celebrate and Visualize the Impossible

Ordinary people believe only in the possible. Extraordinary people visualize not what is possible or probable, but rather what is possible. And by visualizing the impossible, they begin to see it as possible.

Celebrate and Let Go of Your Emotional Baggage

Carrying your negative emotional baggage requires energy that could be put to much better use – say goodbye to it, let it go, and get on with your life.

Celebrate Failure and Opportunity

Failure is simply the opportunity to begin again, this time more intelligently.

Celebrate Your Future

My will shall shape the future. Whether I fail or succeed shall be no man's doing but my own. I can clear any obstacle before me or can be lost in the maze. My choice; my responsibility. Win or lose; only I hold the key to my destiny.

149

Celebrate Positive Goals

Keep working towards your goal and you will always be closer to your goal today than you were yesterday.

Celebrate Because Happiness Is Controlling Your Thoughts

As soon as you recognize that you can control your thoughts happiness will come within your reach.

Celebrate and Learn from mistakes so I

So, I learn from my mistakes. It's a very painful way to learn, but without pain, the old saying is there's no gain. You miss a lot of opportunities by making mistakes, but that's part of it: knowing that you're not shut out forever, and that there's a goal you still can reach.

Celebrate and be Excellent in Habits

We are what we repeatedly do. Excellence, then, is not an act, but a habit.

Celebrate the Attitude You Bring to Life

Your living is determined not so much by what life brings to you as by the attitude you bring to life; not so much by what happens to you as by the way your mind looks at what happens.

Called – *"Blessed are the peacemakers, for they will be called children of God."* (Matthew 5:9).

Equipped – *"All Scripture is God-breathed and is useful for teaching, rebuking, correcting and training in righteousness, so that the servant of God may be thoroughly equipped for every good work."* (2 Timothy 3:16-17).

Loved – *"No, in all these things we are more than conquerors through him who loved us,"* (Romans 8:37a).

Extraordinary – *"Now we have this treasure in clay jars, so that this extraordinary power may be from God and not from us."* (2 Corinthians 4:7).

Beautiful – *"And how can anyone preach unless they are sent? As it is written: "How beautiful are the feet of those who bring good news!""* (Romans 10:15).

Radiant – *"The precepts of the LORD are right, giving joy to the heart. The commands of the LORD are radiant, giving light to the eyes."* (Psalms 19:8).

Anointed – *"The Spirit of the Lord is upon me, because he hath anointed me to preach the gospel to the poor; he hath sent me to heal the* *brokenhearted, to preach deliverance to the captives, and recovering of sight to the blind, to set at liberty them that are bruised."* (Luke 4:18).

Transformed – *"We all, with unveiled faces, are reflecting the glory of the Lord and are being transformed into the same image from glory to glory; this is from the Lord who is the Spirit."* (2 Corinthians 3:18).

"That in every thing ye are enriched by him, in all utterance, and in all knowledge; Even as the testimony of Christ was confirmed in you: So that ye come behind in no gift; waiting for the coming of our Lord Jesus Christ: Who shall also confirm you unto the end, that ye may be blameless in the day of our Lord Jesus Christ." (1 Corinthians 1:5-8).

CHAPTER 21

A Special Treasure Chest

2 Corinthians 4:7, *"But we have this treasure in earthen vessels that the Excellency of the power may be of God, and not of us."* A treasure chest is a box filled with valuable items. The item in the treasure box may not have a high monetary value, but the things are dear to those who possess them. Dreaming of a

treasure chest is a symbol of something that you want to hold close to your heart and keep safe, either something with sentimental value or a precious item that you want to keep secret. If you dream of putting something in a treasure chest, this indicates possession or even an idea that you want to keep safe and keep close to you. Each of us owns a wealth of priceless treasures, treasures that must be safeguarded and preserved.

"Now, therefore, if you will indeed obey my voice and keep my covenant, then you shall be a special treasure to me above all people: for all the earth is mine." (Exodus 19:5).

Each of us are created as a unique treasure to God. Even though we were born in sin and sharpened in iniquity, God still considers us precious. Our Creator puts value in us, and His heart is towards us. We are His people and the sheep of His pasture. A shepherd takes extraordinary care of their sheep. Love will cause a shepherd to leave the ninety-nine and search for one lost sheep. We are the apple of God's eye and His precious treasure in the earth.

Within each of us, there is something that makes our presence valuable. Perhaps it is a kind spirit or a generous heart. Our internal treasures are housed in our character. Maybe you are affectionate, brave, cheerful, faithful, grateful,

154

honest, nurturing, peaceful and trustworthy.

These are all valuable treasures that the world needs. Know that you are a gift to the world, that God wants to unwrap for His glory!

CHAPTER 22

The Ultimate Transformation

In this final chapter I'd like to share some thoughts surrounding what I call the ultimate transformation. I've tried to show in this writing how the power of God can transform any situation in your life into something good. We may not always see the good outcome immediately, but like most things in life, we must wait. When the pressure and troubles of life drift our way, it's not easy to stand against the billowing currents that come to destroy us. But our foundation in the Lord will stand forever.

2 Timothy 2:19a says, *"Nevertheless the foundation of God standeth sure, having this seal, The Lord knoweth them that are his."*

Our hope for today and our strength for tomorrow rest in the Sure Foundation and that foundation is Christ. The trials and temptation of life are necessary for us to grow and become spiritual nature. Trials and temptations are necessary for developing our faith and trust in God.

"Blessed [is] the man that endureth temptation: for when he is tried, he shall receive the crown of life, which the Lord hath promised to them that love him." (James 1:12).

"Beloved, think it not strange concerning the fiery trial which is to try you, as though some strange thing happened unto you." (1 Peter 4:12).

Our ultimate desire should be that our lives be conformed to the image of Christ. We must press our way through the valley, and we must put on the whole armor of God that we might be able to stand.

158

"Wherefore take unto you the whole armor of God, that ye may be able to withstand in the evil day, and having done all, to stand." (Ephesians 6:13).

Like the butterfly, our lives are being changed and developed gradually on our journey. As seasons change, so do we but through God's grace, we are more than conquerors. He is the solid ground that we can stand on.

The Solid Rock

My hope is built on nothing less
Than Jesus' blood and righteousness;
I dare not trust the sweetest frame,
But wholly lean on Jesus' name.
On Christ, the solid Rock, I stand
All other ground is sinking sand.
When darkness veils His lovely face,
I rest on His unchanging grace;
In every high and stormy gale,
My anchor holds within the veil.
On Christ, the solid Rock, I stand;
All other ground is sinking sand.
His oath, His covenant, and blood
Support me in the whelming flood;
When all around my soul give way,

He then is all my Hope and Stays.

On Christ, the solid Rock, I stand;

All other ground is sinking sand.

When He shall come with trumpet sound,

Oh, may I then in Him be found,

Clothed in His righteousness alone,

Faultless to stand before the throne!

On Christ, the solid Rock, I stand;

All other ground is sinking sand.

(Edward Mote).

The female butterfly lay's the seed upon a green leaf. We must let the seed of the Word grow in us by reading, studying and praying for understanding and wisdom. God's Word is a live seed.

"Now the parable is this: The seed is the Word of God." (Luke 8:11).

"Having been born again, not of corruptible seed but incorruptible, through the Word of God which lives and abides forever." (1 Peter 1:23).

Seeds contain life but they must be planted in the heart. A few weeks ago, someone left a pack of flower seeds on my desk. The seeds were tiny. The uniqueness of each seed that

God creates is wondrous, just as we too are unique. As a seed begins to grow, it will push up dirt, rocks and whatever stands in its way. Whatever the stumbling block is, God's Word planted in our heart can move mountains. However; God is not on our time clock. Seeds takes time to produce, and we must wait on God to develop us. No one expects a seed to produce a harvest the same day that seed is planted. God does not expect change overnight. The seed of the Word will be at work even when we get weak. Spending time in the God's Word will help us on our journey in being transformed like the butterfly shedding its' cocoon before release.

Philippians 3:8-11 says, *"More than that, I count all things to be loss in view of the surpassing value of knowing Christ Jesus my Lord, for whom I have suffered the loss of all things, and count them but rubbish so that I may gain Christ, and may be found in Him, not having a righteousness of my own derived from the Law, but that which is through faith in Christ, the righteousness which comes from God on the basis of faith, that I may know Him and the power of His resurrection and the fellowship of His sufferings, being conformed to His death."*

ACKNOWLEDGMENTS

To my Lord and savior Jesus Christ I give glory, honor, and praise. I am grateful for His loving kindness, tender mercy, and compassion that have been poured out on me each day and especially during this writing. I praise God for helping me navigate through the seasons of life and for adopting me into the family of God.

There are many people that I'd like to acknowledge. I begin with honor to my parents' Mattie, and William Whitehead, Sister Delores Hunt and son Phillip Nathaniel Wade II, of whom have always encouraged me. Their lives are a reflection of God's goodness.

To my spiritual father Pastor Jerry Sanders, thank you for helping me understand the growth process necessary for answering the call and assignment God has placed on my life. Your preaching and teaching have changed my life.

Acknowledgements

To my sisters in Christ Evangelist Marjorie Long, Evangelist, Odessa McNeil, Dr. Lakita Long, Jacqueline Miller and Reverend Doctor Dominique Robinson, Reverend Angelita Clifton and Reverend Joyce McDonald, thank you for seeing in me what needed to be pulled out and helping me along the way.

To my dear cousins' Patricia Brown who walked with me from the early days of ministry with continual support and Missionary Theresa Coney whose faithful prayers never ceased. Thank you.

I thank God for introducing me to Shanene Higgins of Higgins Publishing. Shanene has the Spirit of God and is sensitive to the voice of God. Our relationship was divinely purposed. Higgins Publishing provided outstanding service right from the beginning. *Renew Your Mind & Transform Your Life* will be presented to the readers with the spirit of excellence. I am blessed to know Shanene as a friend and business partner.

To all who were willing to share their stories, time and prayers I *Thank you.*

To God be the Glory!

In His Service,
Love Clara

INDEX

Index

Index

Index

Index

Index

Index

Index

ABOUT THE AUTHOR

For more than 25 years in ministry, Clara has dedicated her life to building up the body of believers and sharing the power of a transformed life with those outside of Christ. Her mission has always been to be an impactful servant to all of those who she encounters both inside and out of church walls. Clara has a passion for helping women who are sitting in the sanctuary wounded. Clara exercises a commitment to her community by sharing her time and talent in ways that benefit the community and the individuals involved in her various programs catered toward the growth of self and in the body of Christ.

Clara was born in Tifton, Georgia and migrated to New Jersey in 1958. She earned her Bachelor's degree from Lighthouse Christian College in Bebe, Arkansas 1998. Clara continued her education at Jamison Christian College in Philadelphia, Pennsylvania where she earned her Master's degree in Christian Education. Clara believes that all people have the capacity to accomplish extraordinary things and that every adult has the responsibility to nurture young people who struggle with life on a day to day basis.

She is the originator of Life Path Today seminars and "In-Focus" workshops. Clara, through the help of the Holy Spirit, was guided to develop In-Focus workshops "Facing Our Challenges Using Scripture" that lays the foundation for Christian living. Without a proper foundation she firmly believes that is impossible to build a structure for life that will stand the many tests of life. The programs are especially designed for young women as they transition to adulthood as many are led astray by roads of life that are self-led opposed to Christ led. She believes that everyone must know who they are in Christ and celebrate the treasure they possess.

She currently serves as a motivational speaker for a women's correctional institution in New Jersey as well as an inspirational speaker for teen and adult women who are living in homeless shelters.

In 1996 Clara was nominated as Woman of the Year by the NAACP for her outstanding contribution to her community. Clara is a Spirit-filled & spirit led exhorter who passionately embraces women who are hurting and offers them healing through her personal stories and the word of God. She has dedicated her life to serving God and His people for more than 30 years. Clara is a powerful woman of God, mother, mentor, teacher and humanitarian. Her gift brings clear insight and understanding which directs people to their purpose and destiny.

Her passion, authenticity and humility marks her as a minister of the Gospel. The Holy Spirit exercises her gift in special ways to create the best conditions for God to heal, deliver and set free those who are held captive and broken by life's circumstances. She is continually humbled by the opportunities granted to her and prays that God will continue to keep her in the very palm of His Almighty hand.

Clara has been blessed with one son Phillip who lives in Houston, Texas.